Learning
Structures

Payne, Ruby K., Ph.D.
    Learning Structures. Second revised edition.
Ruby K. Payne © 2001, 121 pp.
    Bibliography pp. 118-119
    ISBN 0-9647437-1-X

Ruby K. Payne. Ph.D.

Learning
Structures

aha!
Process, Inc.

A Framework for Understanding Poverty

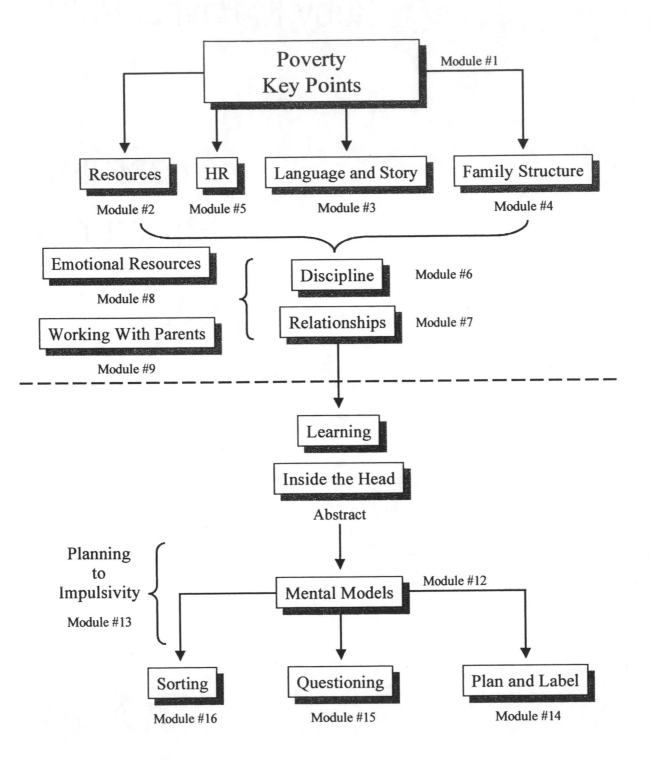

C*ontents*

MODULE 10

BUILDING LEARNING STRUCTURES: OVERVIEW

USING INPUT STRATEGIES IN THE CLASSROOM

In the classroom, input strategies can be embedded into five tasks: (1) plan to control impulsivity; (2) plan and label for academic tasks; (3) use mental models; (4) sort, using patterns and criteria; and (5) do question making. When these five tasks are done with material, the student can learn.

Learning Structures

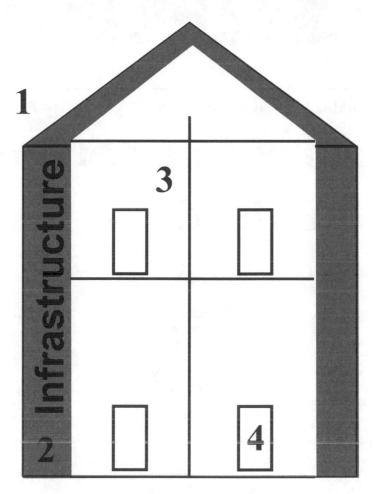

1. Structure (discipline)
2. Cognitive strategies (processes)
3. Conceptual frameworks
4. Sorting mechanisms
   (important from unimportant)

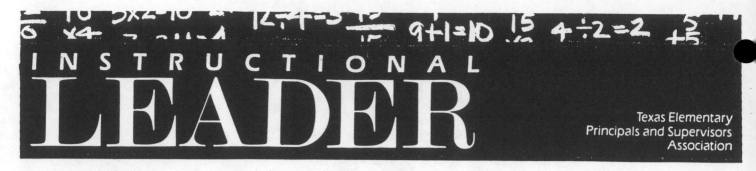

INSTRUCTIONAL LEADER

Texas Elementary
Principals and Supervisors
Association

Volume IX, No. 3

May 1996

Understanding and Working With Students and Adults from Poverty, Part 2:

Building Learning Structures Inside the Head

By Ruby Payne, Ph.D.
Director of Professional Development, Goose Creek CISD

Actual phone conversations:

"Ruby, we got our TAAS data back. I cried and cried. I don't know what else to do. I did everything I know how to do. What is wrong with me? With my teaching? Maybe I should just quit and do something else. "

"I know we are going to get our 'bubble kids' through the TAAS. But as the subpopulation score requirements climb, what are we going to do with the others? Those students that are two and three years behind?"

Teaching is outside the head; learning is inside the head. Every individual has a brain but not everyone has a developed mind. The work of Feuerstein, an Israeli educator who successfully worked for nearly 50 years with students whose mental development was delayed, developed mental prowess through a process of mediation. Mediation involves three things: pointing out the stimuli (what the indi-

vidual is to give attention to), giving it meaning, and providing a strategy.

Mediation occurs through language and direct teaching. Mediation builds learning structures in the head, which allow the learner to accept and process the information. A teacher can teach a perfect lesson, but if the student does not have the structures for accepting and using the information, a great deal of the lesson is lost. Through direct instruction, the undeveloped and under-developed parts of the learning structure can be built.

There are four parts of the structure that must be inside a head before a learner can accept the information. To simply represent these four structures, Figure 1 (on page two) will be used.

Quite simply, these four structures are 1) a structure for data and a structure for the discipline; 2) cognitive strategies or processes; 3) conceptual frameworks (schema); and 4) sorting mechanisms.

The First Structure

The first structure is an organized mechanism for data. In an analogy to a house, it is the studs and foundation—the very things that hold the structure intact and make it a struc-

ture. In an analogy to a computer, it is the hardware itself. It is the organ of the brain that accepts data and structures it. Everything in the universe has structure and is to a certain extent, defined by that structure. The mind is, to some extent, defined by the brain.

In addition, a student needs a structure for each discipline. Structures in disciplines tend to be underlying principles. For example, the key underlying principle in math is to assign order and value to the universe. In chemistry, the key underlying principle is bonding; in algebra, it is solving for the unknown. When the key underlying principle is understood, then the whole discipline has a structure or a way to place data.

The Second Structure: Cognitive Strategies

The second learning structure is cognitive strategies. Feuerstein iden-

© aha! Process, Inc. • (800) 424-9484

Figure 1

Learning Structures

KEY

1) Structure

2) Cognitive Strategies (processes)

3) Conceptual frameworks

4) Sorting mechanisms— important from unimportant

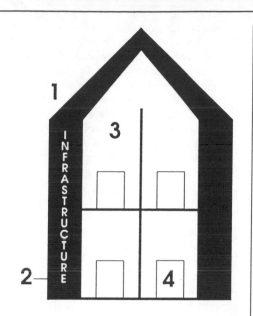

tified several strategies or processes that an individual must successfully have in order to deal with any piece of data. Feuerstein found that students missed much of the original data (up to 50 percent) when the cognitive strategies were not fully or only partially developed.

These strategies are analogous to the infrastructure of a house—the plumbing system, heating system, electrical system, sewage system, etc. In a house, it is when the systems are not working that we realize our reliance upon them. In a computer, these strategies are analogous to the software. Any individual who has worked with a malfunctioning software package knows the importance of this part of the structure.

Feuerstein identified student characteristics when these strategies are missing. The strategies have been restated in the positive, i.e., what students can do when these strategies are present. In the mind, these cognitive strategies are the following:

Input Strategies

Input is defined as the "quantity and quality of the data gathered."

1. Use planning behaviors.
2. Focus perception on a specific stimulus.
3. Control impulsivity.
4. Explore data systematically.
5. Use appropriate and accurate labels.
6. Organize space with stable systems of reference.
7. Orient data in time.
8. Identify constancies across variations.
9. Gather precise and accurate data.
10. Consider two sources of information at once.
11. Organize data (parts of a whole).
12. Visually transport data.

Elaboration Strategies

Elaboration strategies are defined as the "use of the data."

1. Identify and define the problem.
2. Select relevant cues.
3. Compare data.
4. Select appropriate categories of time.
5. Summarize data.
6. Project relationships of data.
7. Use logical data.
8. Test hypothesis.
9. Build inferences.
10. Make a plan using the data.
11. Use appropriate labels.
12. Use data systematically.

Output Strategies

Output is defined as the "communication of the data."

1. Communicate clearly the labels and process.
2. Visually transport data correctly.
3. Use precise and accurate language.
4. Control impulsive behavior.

What do these strategies mean?

Mediation builds these strategies. When these strategies are not present, they can be built. Typically in school, we begin teaching at the elaboration level, i.e., the use of the data. When students do not understand, we reteach these strategies but do not revisit the quality and quantity of the data gathered.

In order to better understand input strategies, each is explained in more detail. Typically, input strategies are not directly taught, because we do not know to teach them. The assumption is that all students have them. However, for unmediated students, these strategies must be taught directly.

Input strategies

(quantity and quality of data)

Using planning behaviors includes goal setting, identifying the procedures in the task, identifying the parts of the task, assigning time to the task(s), and identifying the quality of the work necessary to complete the task.

Focusing perception on a specific stimulus is the strategy of seeing every detail on the page or in the environment. It is the strategy of identifying everything noticed by the five senses.

Controlling impulsivity is the strategy of stopping action until thinking about the task is done. There is a direct correlation with impulsivity control and improved behavior and achievement.

Exploring data systematically means that a strategy is employed to procedurally and systematically go through every piece of data. Numbering is a way to go systematically through data. Highlighting each piece of data can be another method.

Using appropriate and accurate labels is the use of precise words and vocabulary to identify and explain. If a student does not have specific words to use, then his or her ability to retrieve and use information is severely limited. It is not enough that a student can do a task, he/she must also be able to label the procedures, tasks and processes so that the task can be successfully repeated each time and analyzed at a metacognitive level. Metacognition is the ability to think about one's thinking. To do so, labels must be attached. Only when labels are attached can the task be evaluated and therefore improved.

Organizing space with stable systems of reference is crucial to success in math. It means that up, down, right, left, across, horizontal, vertical, diagonal, etc. are understood. It means that an individual can identify what the position of an item is with labels. It means that an individual can organize space. For example. if an individual does not have this strategy, then it is virtually impossible to tell a "p", "b" and "d" apart. The only differentiation is the orientation in space.

Orienting data in time is the strategy of assigning abstract values to time and the measurement of time. This strategy is crucial for identifying cause and effect, for determining sequence, and for predicting consequences.

Identifying constancies across variations is the strategy of knowing what always remains the same and what changes. For example, if you do not know what always makes a square a square, you cannot identify constancies. It allows one to define things, to recognize a person or an object, and to compare and contrast. This strategy allows cursive writing to be read with all of its variations. I asked a group of fifth-grade students I was working with this question: "If you saw me tomorrow, what about me would be the same and what would be different?" Many of the students had difficulty with that strategy.

Gathering precise and accurate data is the strategy of using accurate labels, identifying the orientation in time and in space, knowing the constancies, and exploring the data systematically.

Considering two sources of information at once is the strategy of visually transporting data accurately, identifying the constancies and variations, and exploring the data systematically. When that is done, then precise and accurate labels need to be assigned .

Organizing data (parts of a whole) involves exploring data systematically, organizing space, identifying constancies and variations, and labeling the parts and the whole with precise words.

Visually transporting data is when the eye picks up the data, carries it accurately to the brain, examines it for constancies and variations, and labels the parts and whole. If a student cannot visually transport, then he often cannot read, has difficulty with basic identification of anything, and cannot copy.

Elaboration and output strategies tend to be fairly well understood in schools, because that is where the teaching tends to occur. Feuerstein developed well over 100 instruments to use to build these strategies in the brain.

The Third Structure: Conceptual Frameworks

Conceptual frameworks are the part of the structure that stores and retrieves data. In the house, it is analogous to the rooms. In most houses, rooms are identified by function—the bedroom, the living room, the kitchen, the bathroom, etc.

In a computer, the analogy is to the files. In an oversimplification of conceptual frameworks, they might look something like Figure 2.

These frameworks need the general or abstract words so that categories can be made for information, like the files in a computer or the rooms in a house. Development goes from the specific and concrete to the abstract and general.

At least two quick ways are available to diagnose the development and accessibility of conceptual frameworks. First, if a student gives an example rather than a definition, you know that the concrete part of the framework is available, but the abstract part is not. To store much information, abstract words are necessary to assign and label the categories. Casual register has very little abstract terminology, so students who do not have access to formal register have difficulty with assigning things to categories.

The second way to diagnose conceptual frameworks is whether a student can ask a question syntactically. For example, the student will ask, "Don't you have any more?" If a student makes a statement but tonally infers it is a question, e.g. "You don't have any more?" then a high probability exists that the student has a low reading comprehension score

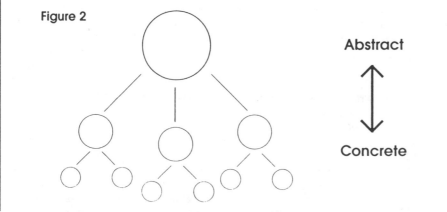

Figure 2

Abstract

↕

Concrete

(Palinscar), and the student is unable to access the stored information with any repeated success. If you have a student who cannot answer the test questions unless they are exactly the same as the review questions, then you have a student who cannot access their conceptual frameworks or "files."

Quite simply, if a student cannot ask questions syntactically, his ability to learn is significantly reduced, because he cannot identify what he does not know nor can he systematically access what he does know.

There are several ways to build in conceptual frameworks, but one of the most successful methods is reciprocal teaching by Anne Palinscar. Another successful method is to make students write their own multiple choice questions using question stems. Vocabulary development is yet another. *Tactics for Thinking* (Marzano) has several activities that assist in this development.

The Fourth Structure: Models for Sorting

Before any data can be stored so that it can be found, some method for sorting the data must exist. Sorting the data simply means identifying what is important and what is not important. Sorting the data is analogous to the door on the room. It is what allows the entrance and exit to the file. On the computer, it is the click of the cursor on the file or the pathway.

Students have difficulty sorting information, particularly nonfiction text, because we do not teach how to sort important from unimportant, except as a summary skill. Furthermore, if the student uses a random, episodic story structure, memory is often assigned on the basis of what has emotional significance. Because many students do not have a method for sorting information, they try to remember as much as possible, which is very ineffective.

Skilled learners sort text by the organizational pattern or structure of the text. For example, if an article is

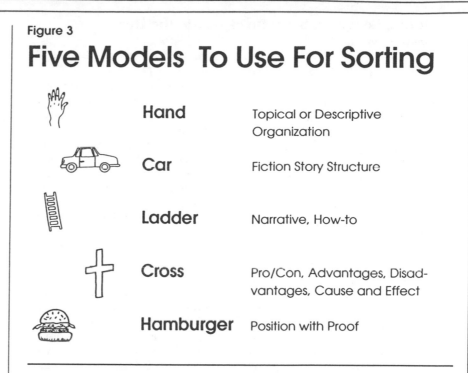

Figure 3

Five Models To Use For Sorting

Hand	Topical or Descriptive Organization
Car	Fiction Story Structure
Ladder	Narrative, How-to
Cross	Pro/Con, Advantages, Disadvantages, Cause and Effect
Hamburger	Position with Proof

Figure 4

Fiction Story Structure

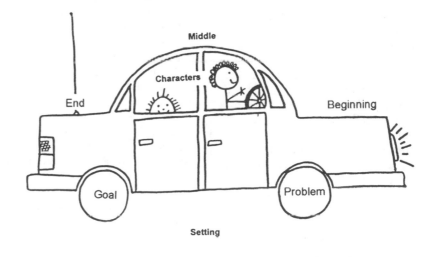

about the causes and effects of the Civil War, then the reader would sort for causes and effects. If the text compares and contrasts a given topic, then the reader would want to remember what was alike and what was different. We have given students graphic ways to organize their writing, but we have not given them the models to sort text. Basically, the majority of text

that students see in schools can be represented by one of five models. Students are simply taught how to identify the five models and sort text with the five models.

In addition, other teaching techniques are available to assist with sorting. Project Read has several good ideas.

Please turn to page 12

© aha! Process, Inc. • (800) 424-9484

Building Learning Structures Inside the Head
continued from page 5

continued from page 5

The Five Models to Use For Sorting

In order to remember, the mind must sort through information and store what is important and discard what is not important. In order to remember the important parts of text, the mind needs to sort against the structure of the text.

We have traditionally used graphic organizers to help students write text. Being able to sort the important from the unimportant during reading is the flip side of that coin. *Using models to help students sort text gives them a way to remember organizational patterns and to identify what is important.* The graphic organizers need to be simple so they are easy to remember. The five symbols in Figure 3 can be used. Any five can be used. Most text that students see in school fits one of these patterns.

How does a teacher use these with students? Give students a piece of text to read and one of the five models. Initially, choose the model that fits the organizational pattern of the text. Put students into pairs. Have them select the most important information and write it into an outline of the model. When finished, use a transparency and help students identify the most important information. Each student should add to his or her written model the information that has been missed.

Because the TAAS test has so much nonfiction text, students have difficulty because they want to sort using the fiction story structure (see Figure 4) and so remember the characters, setting and plot. By directly teaching them to sort, students can better select the important information.

Conclusion

The less mediated the student is, the more need the student has for direct instruction in these structures. For several of the reasons I cited in the March *Instructional Leader*, many students from poverty do not have these structures sufficiently in place to do well on the TAAS.

All that means is that we must provide direct instruction to build these in their minds. It means that we trade out some of the activities we use that do not have a great amount of payoff in achievement for those that have a higher payoff. For example, rather than having students answer questions at the end of the chapter, they can compose questions. When a student does not have orientation in space, we embed that as a part of the instruction.

Direct instruction to build these strategies is imperative because of the issue of time. Historically, the reason individuals hired teachers or tutors was to provide the learning more efficiently than the individual could without assistance. Trial and error, as well as experience, can be valuable teachers, but they take more time.

It will be from our interventions with the learning structures that greater strides in student achievement will come. Students who have been traditionally successful in school came to school with learning structures; we built our traditional instructional design around the notion that these would be in place.

But these structures can be built. Someone built them in the minds of students who come to school ready to learn. At school, Feuerstein built them successfully into students who at 12 and 13 years old did not have them. As we reframe our instruction to include their construction, student achievement will increase.

References

Feuerstein, Reuven, et al. (1980). *Instrumental Enrichment: An Intervention Program for Cognitive Modifiability.* Scott, Foresman and Co. Glenview, Illin.

Idol, Lorna and Jones, B.F. (1991). *Educational Values and Cognitive Instruction: Implications for Reform.* Lawrence Erlbaum Associates. Hillsdale, New Jersey.

Marzano, Robert J. and Arrendondo, Daisy. (1986). *Tactics for Thinking.* MCREL. Aurora, Colo.

Palinscar, A.S. and Brown, A.L. (1984). "The reciprocal teaching of comprehension-fostering and comprehension-monitoring activities." *Cognition and Instruction.* 1. (2), 117-125.

Many students from poverty do not have the learning structures sufficiently in place to do well on the TAAS.

AUTHOR NOTE:
Ruby K. Payne, Ph.D., is the director of professional development at Goose Creek CISD in Baytown, Texas. She is also the author of *Poverty: A Framework for Understanding and Working With Students and Adults from Poverty.* Contact her by phone at 713-424-9151 and by fax at 713-424-2297.

Cognitive Strategies*

INPUT:
quantity and quality of data gathered

1. Use planning behaviors.
2. Focus perception on specific stimulus.
3. Control impulsivity.
4. Explore data systematically.
5. Use appropriate and accurate labels.
6. Organize space using stable systems of reference.
7. Orient data in time.
8. Identify constancies across variations.
9. Gather precise and accurate data.
10. Consider two sources of information at once.
11. Organize data (parts of a whole).
12. Visually transport data.

1. Identify and define the problem.
2. Select relevant cues.
3. Compare data.
4. Select appropriate categories of time.
5. Summarize data.
6. Project relationships of data.
7. Use logical data.
8. Test hypothesis.
9. Build inferences.
10. Make a plan using the data.
11. Use appropriate labels.
12. Use data systematically.

ELABORATION:
efficient use of the data

OUTPUT:
communication of elaboration and input

1. Communicate clearly the labels and process.
2. Visually transport data correctly.
3. Use precise and accurate language.
4. Control impulsive behavior.

*adapted from the work of Reuven Feuerstein

Metacognition

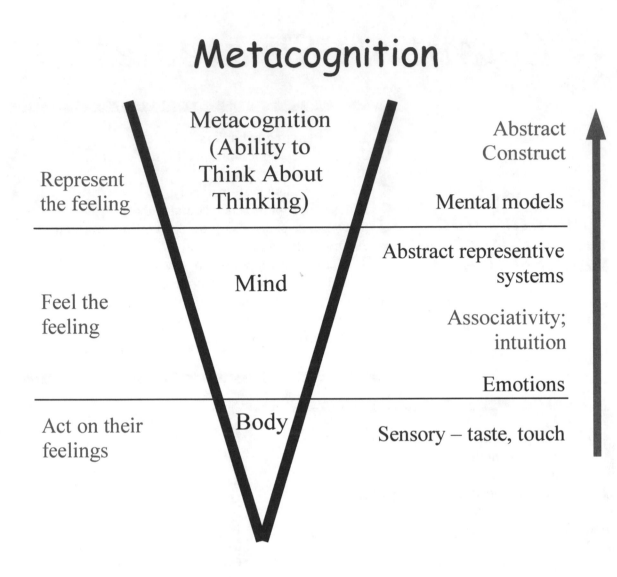

MODULE 11

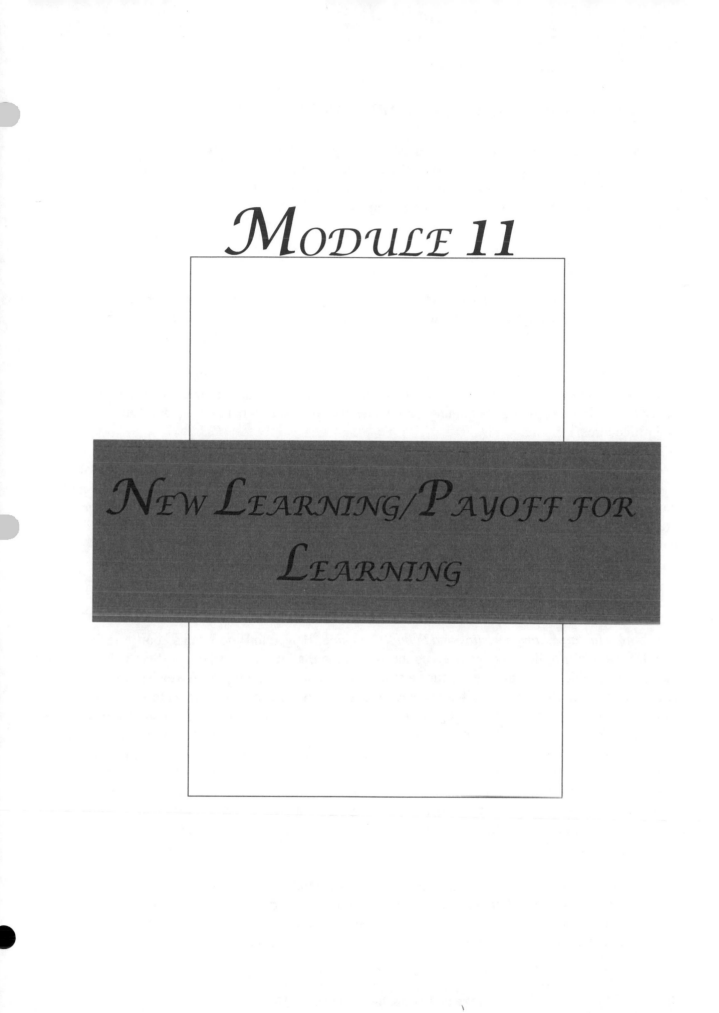

NEW LEARNING/PAYOFF FOR LEARNING

NEW LEARNING AND THE PAYOFF FOR LEARNING

Two concepts that are essential to working successfully with students from poverty are: (1) the fact that many students are new learners to the abstract and (2) that because they come into school without the "ready to learn" attributes that are expected, schools must maximize the time they have to "catch up" the students who come in "behind."

NEW LEARNERS

Many students are new learners to the abstract. Success on the street is a very concrete reality; success in school is a very abstract reality. Because casual register does not have the number of abstract words that formal register does, vocabulary is often cited as a primary issue.

There is a process any human being goes through when he/she is a new learner. (See p. 21.) What is important to note is that every beginning learner is a novice and, as such, needs a "what" and a "how." In other words, beginning learners need examples of what is to be done and they need procedures.

The other aspect about new learners is the brain research that Caine and Caine cite in their book, *Making Connections*. The brain has at least two memory systems with which to learn: locale and taxon. Taxon memory is used when there is no context (i.e., no experience). So a new learner is in taxon memory. (See p. 23.) What skilled teachers do is teach to both taxon and locale memory.

PAYOFF FOR LEARNING

In his book *Human Characteristics and School Learning*, Benjamin Bloom talks about the four variables that make a difference in the amount of learning that occurs in schools. (See p. 20.) One of the variables is the amount of time a student has to learn something. A key issue in raising achievement in schools is to ask what is being taught and how much time is given to it. Usually, schools are familiar with their pedagogy (how something is being taught – direct instruction, small group, cooperative learning, lab, etc.). When a school knows *what* is being taught and how much time is given to it, then the school can begin to analyze the payoff in learning. For example, I was working with a seventh-grade English teacher who was spending one day a week on spelling. I asked her what percentage of the time she was spending on spelling. She said 20%. I asked her if she was getting a payoff in learning. Was she seeing a 20% increase in correct spelling? Were her test scores higher? Were the students becoming better readers and writers? She said no. Then I asked, "Why do it?"

Generally, the teachers who get higher achievement from students are very clear about which activities affect learning and which ones do not. When teachers direct-teach how to plan, planning and labeling, question making, sorting, and mental models, a higher payoff for learning occurs, and the amount of time it takes to learn something can be reduced.

18

It is possible to
have a brain and
not have a mind.
A brain is
inherited;
a mind is
developed.

Attributed to Reuven Feuerstein

TYPICAL BRAIN NEURON

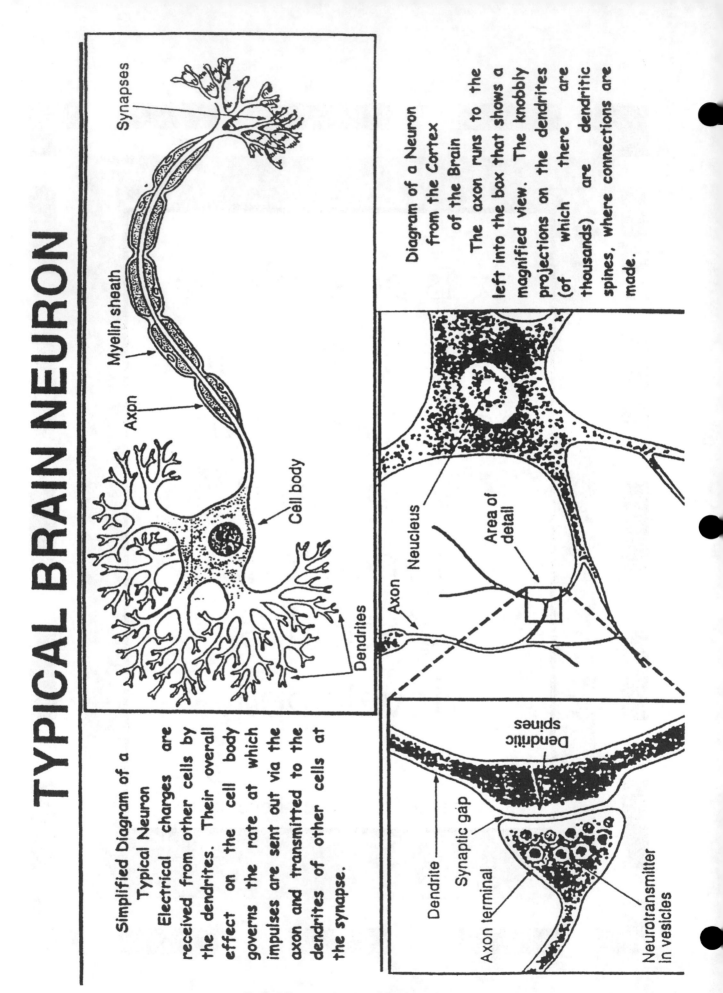

Synapses

Myelin sheath

Axon

Cell body

Dendrites

Simplified Diagram of a Typical Neuron

Electrical charges are received from other cells by the dendrites. Their overall effect on the cell body governs the rate at which impulses are sent out via the axon and transmitted to the dendrites of other cells at the synapse.

Diagram of a Neuron from the Cortex of the Brain

The axon runs to the left into the box that shows a magnified view. The knobbly projections on the dendrites (of which there are thousands) are dendritic spines, where connections are made.

Neucleus

Axon

Area of detail

Dendritic spines

Dendrite

Synaptic gap

Axon terminal

Neurotransmitter in vesicles

Developmental Stages in Learning a Profession

adapted from work of D.C. Berliner and Benjamin Bloom

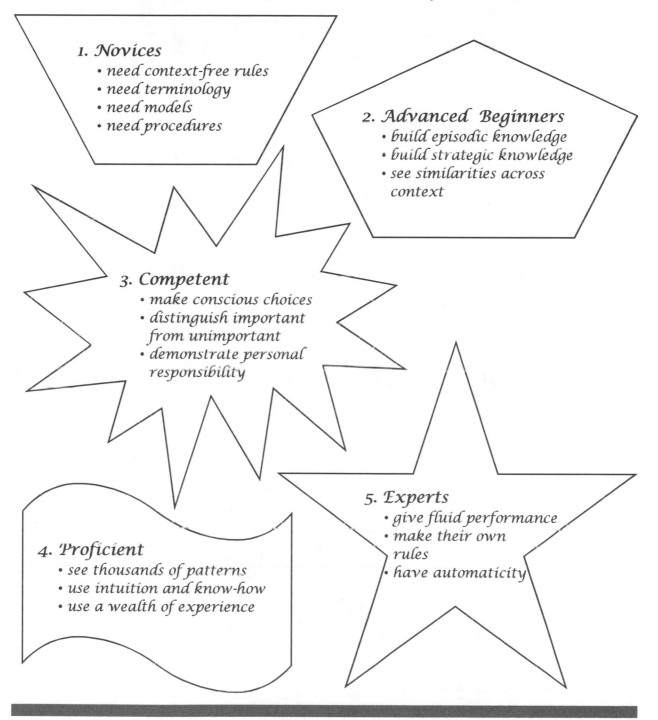

1. Novices
- need context-free rules
- need terminology
- need models
- need procedures

2. Advanced Beginners
- build episodic knowledge
- build strategic knowledge
- see similarities across context

3. Competent
- make conscious choices
- distinguish important from unimportant
- demonstrate personal responsibility

4. Proficient
- see thousands of patterns
- use intuition and know-how
- use a wealth of experience

5. Experts
- give fluid performance
- make their own rules
- have automaticity

MORE ABOUT LEARNING ...

- ♦ When learning occurs, the brain is reorganized, which changes the perceived self.

- ♦ The search for meaning occurs through patterning.

- ♦ Emotions are pivotal to patterning.

Taken from Caine & Caine (1991)

Memory Systems

Taxon	Locale
No context	Context
Memory capacity about five things	Unlimited memory
Requires continuous rehearsal	Loss of accessibility over time
Short-term memory	Long-term memory
Limited to extrinsic motivation	Motivated by novelty, curiosity, expectation (intrinsic)
Specific, habit-like behaviors resistant to change	Updated continuously, flexible
Isolated items	Interconnected, spatial memory
Not connected to meaning	Has meaning motivated by a need to make sense
Acquisition of relatively fixed routes	Initial maps formed quickly Involves sensory activity and emotion; generates personal maps through creation of personal meaning
Route	Map

What develops locale memory?

- Thematic units
- Integrated instruction
- Graphic organizers
- Music, art, sensory data
- Physical movement, color
- Metaphors
- Examples
- Analogies
- Models
- Stories
- Writing
- Emotion
- Choice
- Evaluation tools (rubrics, criteria)

The amount of active participation in the learning (covert or overt) is an excellent index of the quality of instruction for the purpose of predicting or accounting for individual student learning.

Taken from Benjamin Bloom. (1976). *Human Characteristics and School Learning.*

MODULE 12

MENTAL MODELS IN SCIENCE, MATH, SOCIAL STUDIES, LANGUAGE ARTS

MENTAL MODELS

To translate the concrete to the abstract, the mind needs to hold the information in a mental model. A mental model can be a two-dimensional visual representation, a story, a metaphor, or an analogy.

To understand any discipline or field of study, one must understand the mental models that the discipline uses. All disciplines are based on mental models. For example, when an individual builds a house, much discussion and words (the abstract) are used to convey what the finished house (concrete) will be. But between the words and the finished house are blueprints. Blueprints are the translators. Between the three-dimensional concrete house and the abstract words, a two-dimensional visual translates.

When these are directly taught, abstract information can be learned much more quickly because the mind has a way to contain it or hold it.

One of the most important mental models for students to have is a mental model for time that includes a past, present, and future. A mental model for time is critical to understanding cause, effect, consequence, and sequence. Without a model for time, an individual cannot plan. (Please note that there are cultural differences in mental models for time. However, all cultural mental models for time do have a way to address past, present, and future.)

To access a student's mental model, use sketching or ask for a story, analogy, or metaphor.

Sketching is a particularly useful tool in better understanding what a student has stored in terms of mental models. To do sketching with students, have them draw a two-dimensional visual of how they think about a word, an idea, a person, etc.

FIVE EXAMPLES OF MENTAL MODELS

1. Using a symbol system as a mental model for formal register. Project Read has a method for representing formal register in symbols that is simply brilliant. (See p. 34.)

2. Using a visual as a mental model for time, space, and procedure. (See pp. 31-33, 35-43.)

3. Using a story as a mental model. A teacher was having difficulty getting students to round off numbers. So they made up this story. A 5, 6, 7, 8, or 9 is a bully. If I give you the number 167 and ask you to round it off, here's what you will do. The last number is a 7, and 7 is knocking on your door. Because it is a 7, you know it's a bully. There is no fight (0) because you run next door to the 6 and stay there. Because there is one more with the 6, the number becomes a 7, so the rounded-off number is 170.

4. Using an analogy as a mental model.

5. Using a metaphor as a mental model.

Examples of Sketching

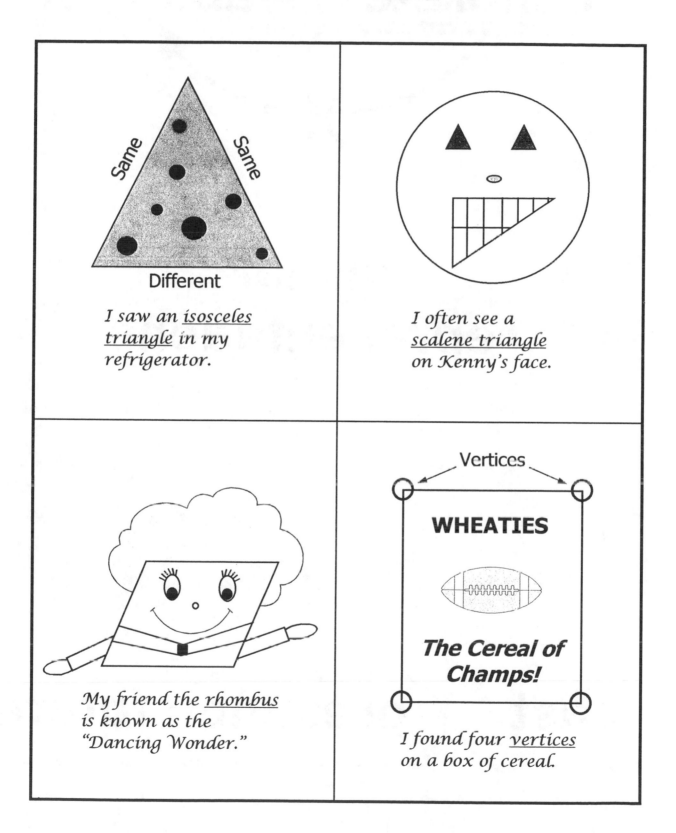

I saw an *isosceles triangle* in my refrigerator.

I often see a *scalene triangle* on Kenny's face.

My friend the *rhombus* is known as the "Dancing Wonder."

I found four *vertices* on a box of cereal.

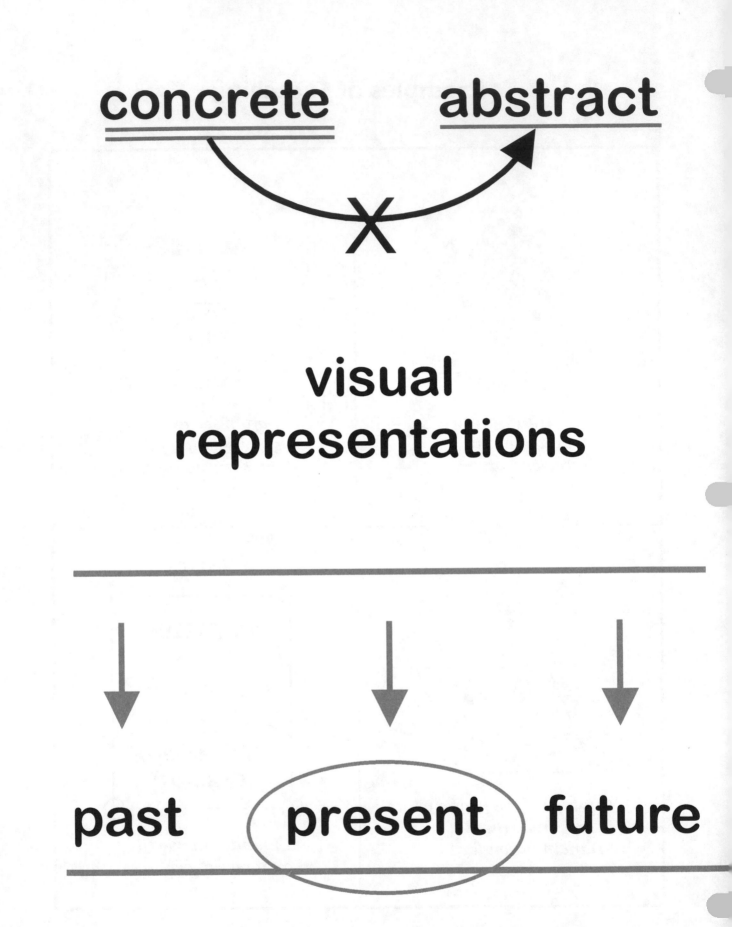

Mental Models for Analogies

TYPES OF ANALOGIES

1. Synonyms

2. Antonyms

3. Indicative

4. Cause/Effect

5. Subsets

6. Degree

7. Function/Purpose

8. Definitional

****

VISUAL ANALOGY

SYNONYM

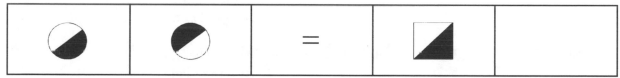

ANTONYM

↓	↑	=	←	

EXAMPLES

1. SYNONYMS   annual / yearly   =   A) ugly / nasty
                                                             B) pretty / good
                                                             C) toads / frogs
                                                             D) often / frequent

2. ANTONYMS   skinny / fat   =   A) sloppy / neat
   B) love / hate
   C) dark / light
   D) adore / dislike

3. INDICATIVE   smile / happy   =   A) wet / slippery
   B) yawn / tired
   C) wink / tease
   D) shiver / hot

4. CAUSE/EFFECT   match / fire   =   A) slip / fall
   B) joke / laugh
   C) bomb / destruction
   D) drop / break

5. SUBSETS   pickup / truck   =   A) country / music
   B) chicken / barbecue
   C) weeds / grass
   D) sedan / car

6. DEGREE   angry / enraged =   A) happy / cheerful
   B) surprised / scared
   C) hungry / starving
   D) upset / annoyed

7. FUNCTION/PURPOSE   oil / lubricate   =   A) clouds / rain
   B) lamp / light
   C) plant / grow
   D) dish / wash

8. DEFINITIONAL   harbor / protect =   A) fantasy / dream
   B) book / read
   C) file / keep
   D) laugh / fun

ANSWERS

1. D   A is incorrect because ugly and nasty do not mean the same. B is wrong for the same reason. C is wrong because toads and frogs are not the same species.

2. A   A is correct because sloppy and neat are opposites and are both adjectives, as skinny and fat are. B and C are opposites but are not adjectives. D is a set of adjectives, but they are not distinct opposites.

3. B   A is not indicative, i.e., just because something is wet does not mean it is slippery. Also, wet is an adjective; smile is either a verb or noun. C is incorrect because while a wink may mean to tease, tease is not an adjective. D is incorrect because shiver does not indicate hot.

4. C   A is incorrect because a slip does not necessarily mean a fall. The same is true of B and D. C is more correct than any of the other choices because it has the same relationship and the same type of relationship.

5. D   In A there is a subset, if country can be considered a type of music; it is not the best choice. In B and C, while chicken is found at a barbecue and weeds are found in grass, neither is a subset of the other.

6. C   A is incorrect because happy and cheerful are synonyms and mean basically the same thing. B is incorrect because it is not a degree relationship but a cause-and-effect one. D is incorrect because annoyed is less intense than upset; the relationship of angry to enraged indicates a relationship of more intensity, not less.

7. B   A is incorrect because the function of clouds is not necessarily to produce rain. C is incorrect because plant and grow are not about function and purpose; growing is something plants do. D is incorrect because the dishes do not function to wash (though there are those who would disagree!).

8. A   B is incorrect because a book is not a definition of read or vice versa. The same is true of C and D.

Mental Model for Formal Register –
Written Expression

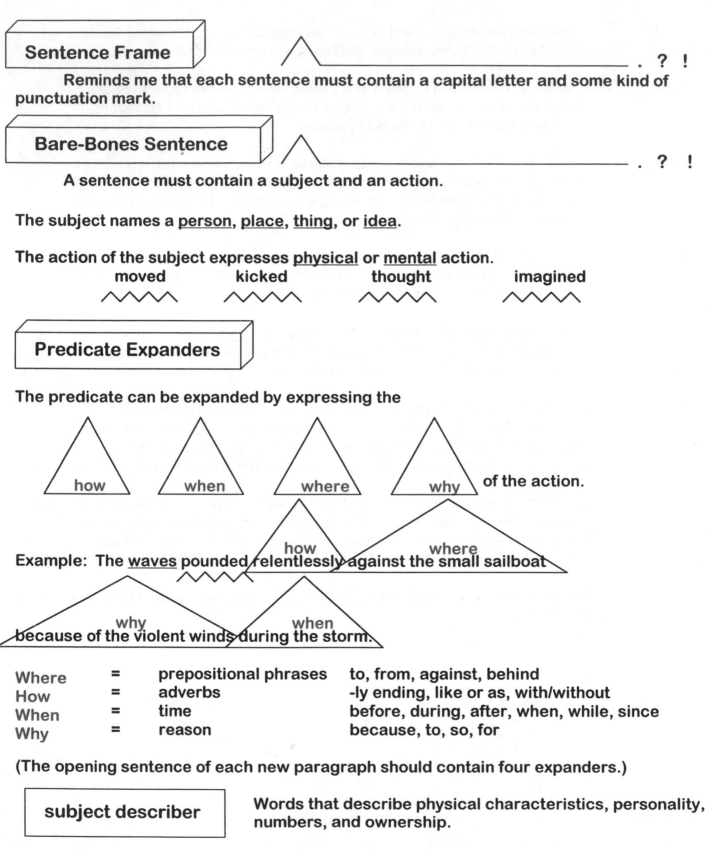

Sentence Frame

_____ . ? !

Reminds me that each sentence must contain a capital letter and some kind of punctuation mark.

Bare-Bones Sentence

_____ . ? !

A sentence must contain a subject and an action.

The subject names a <u>person</u>, <u>place</u>, <u>thing</u>, or <u>idea</u>.

The action of the subject expresses <u>physical</u> or <u>mental</u> action.

   moved   kicked   thought   imagined

Predicate Expanders

The predicate can be expanded by expressing the

how   when   where   why   of the action.

Example: The <u>waves</u> pounded relentlessly against the small sailboat because of the violent winds during the storm.

(how / where / why / when)

Where	=	prepositional phrases	to, from, against, behind
How	=	adverbs	-ly ending, like or as, with/without
When	=	time	before, during, after, when, while, since
Why	=	reason	because, to, so, for

(The opening sentence of each new paragraph should contain four expanders.)

subject describer   Words that describe physical characteristics, personality, numbers, and ownership.

For more information, contact Victoria Green or Mary Lee Enfield at (800) 450-0343.

Which picture shows a reflection (flip) of the figure?

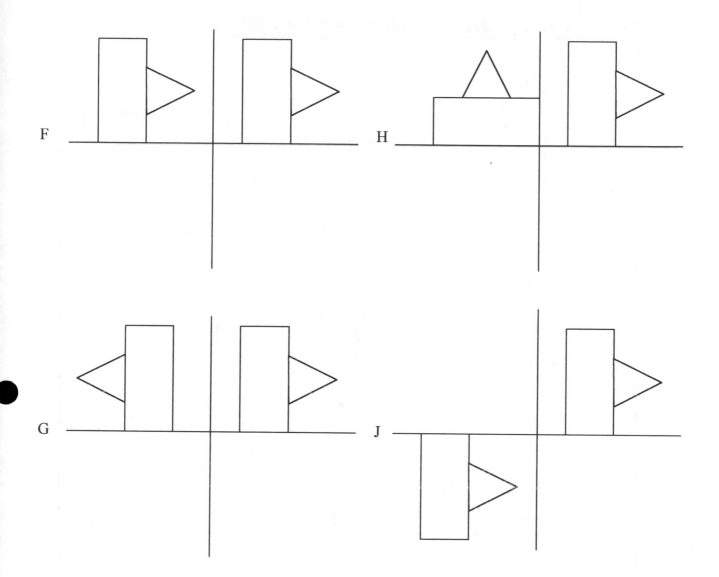

Taken from Texas Assessment of Academic Skills (1996) Grade 5

Mental Model for Space

On which side of the tip of the arrow is the dot?

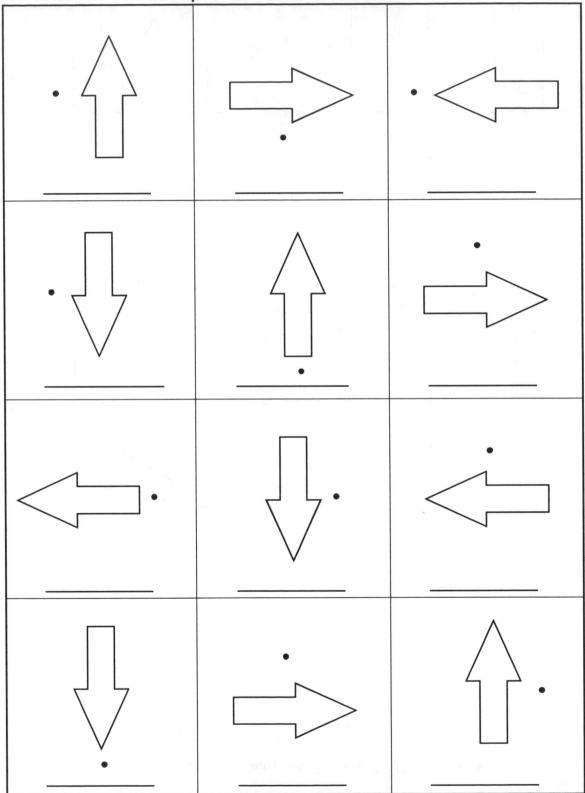

Mental Model in Social Studies

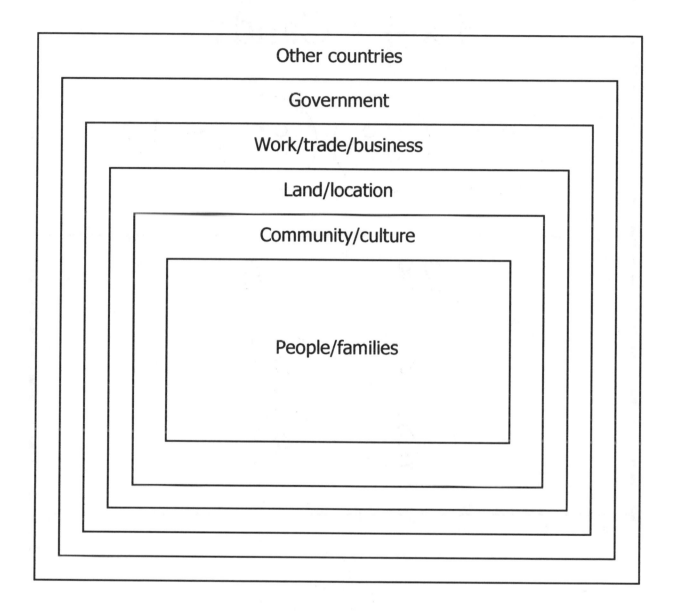

Other countries

Government

Work/trade/business

Land/location

Community/culture

People/families

3 x 4 = Candy

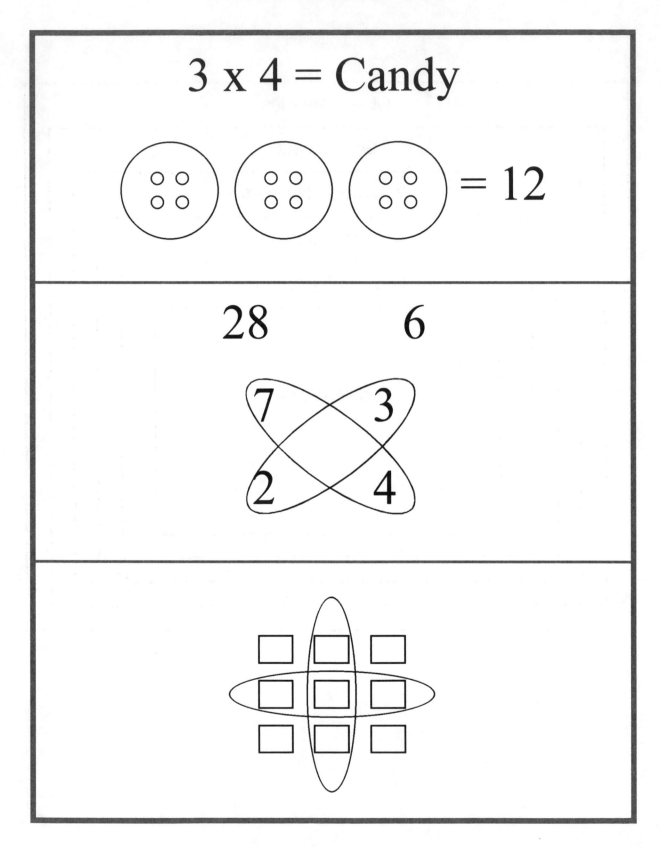

Mental Models in Math

+ Good guy − Bad guy	+ Coming to town − Leaving town	Get
+ + − −	+ − + −	+ − − +

Millions   <u>Thousands</u>

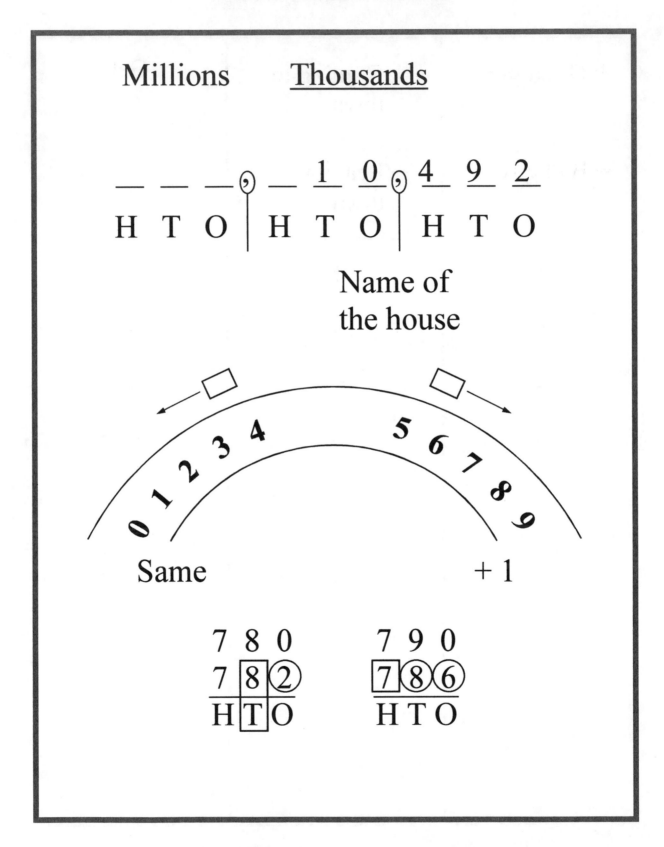

Name of
the house

Same   +1

Planning Backwards

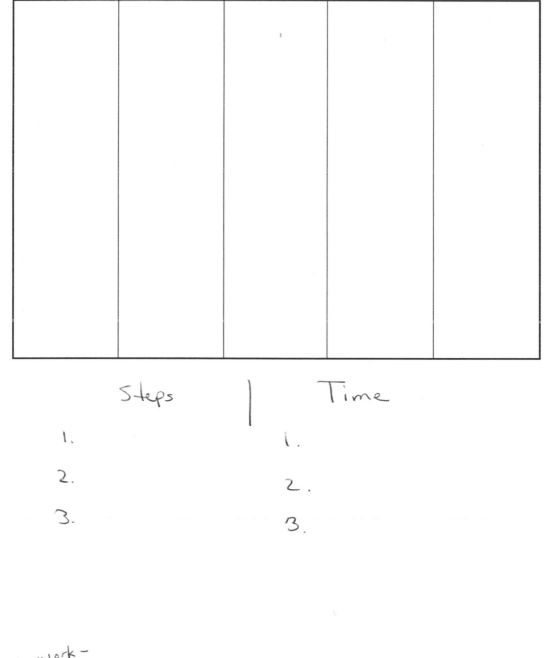

Steps | Time

1.   1.

2.   2.

3.   3.

always have work –
Friday – contract   20% of grade   plan
interest
choice

Draw a map (with pictures) to show how to get from school to your house.

Use symbols to represent objects in space.

Tasks: Draw classroom
Football plays
Relationships

MODULE 13

PLANNING TO CONTROL IMPULSIVITY

PLANNING TO CONTROL IMPULSIVITY

There are several ways to teach impulse control to students. It is important to note that it is the student who does the planning, not the teacher. As long as the teacher does the planning, the student has not had to do the cognitive work. It is also important to note that, generally, planning is effective *only if the plan is written.*

1. **Plan, Do, Review.** There are several variations on this method. Many teachers put the academic tasks on the board. The students keep a learning log. At the beginning of class, they answer the question, "What is your plan for today?" They may write the order in which they are going to do the tasks or may say things like, "I am not going to talk to Robert today." At the end of class, they answer this question, "Did you do your plan? Why or why not?" For younger children, the plans can be in the form of drawn pictures.

2. **Pictures.** Especially for younger students, planning can be taught in the form of pictures. One picture can be of a student who did not plan and another of one who did. It can be as simple as one was happy because he had a plan and got to do what he wanted to do at recess. The other student did not have a plan and did not get to do what she wanted to do at recess. A plan helps you get what you want.

3. **Step Sheets** (p. 47). Step sheets provide procedural information for academic tasks. If students cannot plan, they often do not have procedural self-talk. They tend to do the first few steps and then quit. A step sheet helps them successfully do the task every time.

4. **Planning Backwards** (p. 41). This method of planning has been very successful for many students. Draw a grid with a box for each day the student has before the assignment is due. Label the boxes with the days of the week and dates. Go to the last box – the day the project is due. Below the box make a list of tasks the students must do to finish the assignment. Then ask the students, "What do you have to do the day it is due?" Someone will say, "Hand it in." Then you ask, "What do you have to do the day before it is due?" and often you will get the very first thing that must be done. Eventually, you help the class pace the activities in such a way that the entire project can be done. Then the teacher gives grades two ways: One grade is given regarding the tasks completed each day and the other grade by the final product.

5. **Planning Their Grades** (pp. 48-49). At the beginning of the grading period, the teacher asks students to answer questions about the kinds of grades they want. Then each Friday the teacher gives 15 minutes for the students to record their grades from the week, calculate their averages, and identify what they must do to maintain or bring up their grades.

Classificatory

PARAGRAPH 1   **INTRODUCTION**
* 3+ sentences.
* Rewrite the prompt.
* Give general information and/or an opinion.

PARAGRAPH 2   **ADVANTAGES**
* 8+ sentences.
* Make a statement: "There are advantages to …"
* Write *ADV 1* sentence.
* *Elaborate* using two sentences.
* Write *ADV 2* sentence.
* *Elaborate* using two sentences.
* Make a concluding statement: "There are some advantages to …"

PARAGRAPH 3   **ADVANTAGES OR DISADVANTAGES**
* 8+ sentences.
* Make a statement: "Additionally, there are other advantages to …" or "On the other hand, there are disadvantages to …"
* Write *ADV 3 or DIS 1* sentence.
* *Elaborate* using two sentences.
* Write *ADV 4 or DIS 2* sentence.
* *Elaborate* using two sentences.
* Make a concluding statement.

PARAGRAPH 4   **DISADVANTAGES**
* 8+ sentences.
* Make a statement.
* Write *DIS 3 or DIS 1* sentence.
* *Elaborate* using two sentences.
* Write *DIS 4 or DIS 2* sentence.
* *Elaborate* using two sentences.
* Make a concluding statement.

PARAGRAPH 5   **CONCLUSION**
* 3+ sentences.
* Restate the prompt.
* Give specific information and/or opinions.

Developed by Molly Davis and Julie Heffner

English III – Making the Grade

1. What work have I done well in my English class?

    a.

    b.

    c.

    d.

2. What work have I done poorly in my English class?

    a.

    b.

    c.

    d.

3. I was/was not satisfied with my grade in English III last semester.

    1st _____   2nd _____   3rd _____   Exam _____   Average _____

4. What grade do I realistically believe that I can earn this semester in English III? _____

5. What will I do in my English class to earn that grade?

    a.

    b.

    c.

Spring Semester

Fourth Grading Period   I want to earn _____.

                                  Daily 10%   Quiz 30%   Test 60%

Fifth Grading Period   I want to earn _____.

                                  Daily 10%   Quiz 30%   Test 60%

Sixth Grading Period   I want to earn _____.

                                  Daily 10%   Quiz 30%   Test 60%

I am/am not satisfied with my grade in English III this semester.

     1st _____   2nd _____   3rd _____   Exam _____   Average _____

MODULE 14

PLAN AND LABEL FOR ACADEMIC TASKS

PLAN AND LABEL FOR ACADEMIC TASKS

There are at least four ways to *systematically label* tasks: numbering, lettering, assigning symbols, and color-coding. It is important to note that a systematic approach to the labeling means that fewer pieces of the task are skipped or missed. *For a task to be done correctly, a student must have a plan, procedure, and labels (vocabulary). Labels are the tools the mind uses to address the task.*

There are several ways to teach this. It is easier to begin by using visual activities that have no words. This teaches students that all tasks must have a plan and labels.

1. Reproduce a visual. Give the students a visual to copy (p. 56). Have them fold the paper vertically into four parts (like a fan with only one part showing). Have them draw what is in that part only. Then have them number each line in the original visual. After that, ask them to give that same number to each part of their drawing. Did they get every line? Have them go on to the next section. Then you transfer that to academic tasks. What are all the parts of the task? (Number them and write what each one is.) What is their plan? (In what order are they going to do it, and how will they deal with time?)

2. Change directions on a visual (p. 53). This is an excellent way to get students ready to follow directions on tests, assignments, etc.

3. Plan and label text (pp. 59-60). Have students outline the left-hand edge of text. (You can copy a page of text from a textbook or give them clear transparency sheets to lay over the text.) When the paragraph indents, the student indents. Wherever the line indents, students number inside the indent. Then students find the one word that tells what that paragraph is about and circle it. It becomes a very quick referencing system and also can become a way to summarize. Students are asked to write one sentence with each circled word. The sentences become a summary of the text.

4. Draw visual representations. In math, for example, the problem is drawn as a picture.

5. Develop specific vocabulary with specific tasks (pp. 90-104).

6. Use symbols to label (p. 57-58).

Look at the sample. In each of the two frames, make a new drawing using the changes indicated.

△		
	number color size form	number color size form
◯ ◯ ◯		
	number color size form	number color size form
↑		
	number color size form	number color size form
◇		
	number color size form	number color size form
▢ ▢ ▢		
	number color size form	number color size form
▭		
	number color size form	number color size form

Organization of Dots

OBJECTIVE: Control impulsivity, search systematically, and form a hypothesis.

MATERIALS: Worksheets.

APPLICATIONS:

1. Students must come up with a plan in order to connect the dots.
2. Test the hypothesis in the top row to see if the plan is workable.
3. After working the second row, discuss if the plan needs to be altered – or can it remain the same?

1. Repeat with development of the plan.
   (Notice the elimination of darker dots.)
2. Does that make a difference in the plan?
   If not, why not?

1. Repeat development of a plan.
2. What new problem do we encounter?
3. Does that change our plan?

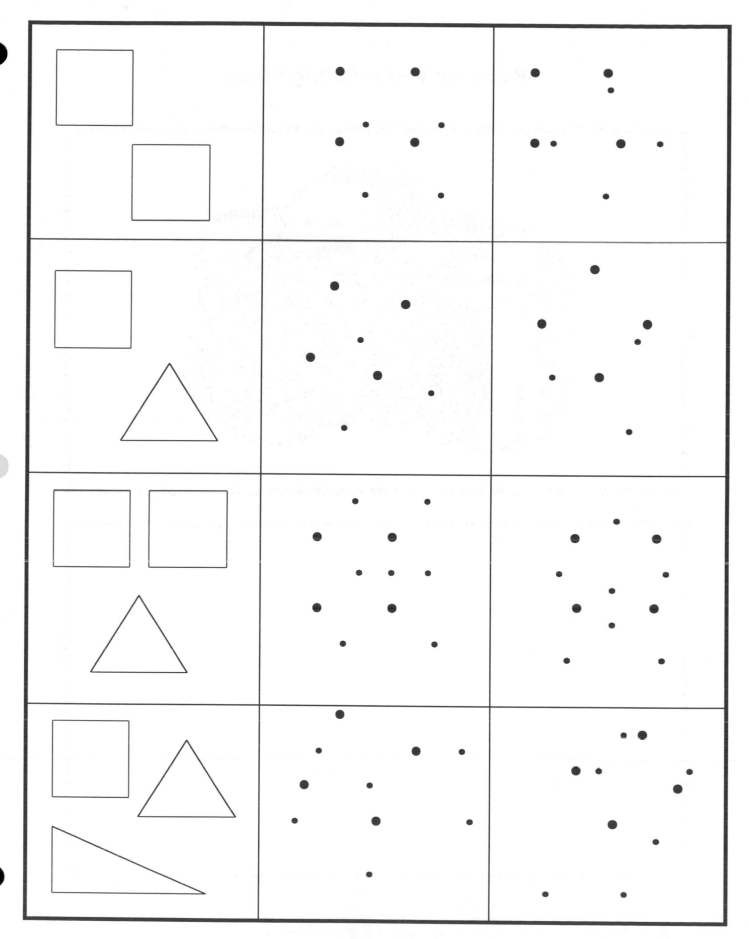

Planning and Labeling Space

Plan and Label in Math

1. 6⌐	Divisor – number of parts in a group
2. ⌐240	Dividend – total number of parts
3. ⌐⊂⊃	Quotient – number of groups
4. 6⌐240	Are there enough parts for a group?
5. 6⌐240	Are there enough parts for a group? If so, how many groups?
6. 4 x 6⌐24 24	See if there are extra parts.

Plan and Label in Science

How (process)	Why (concept)
1. 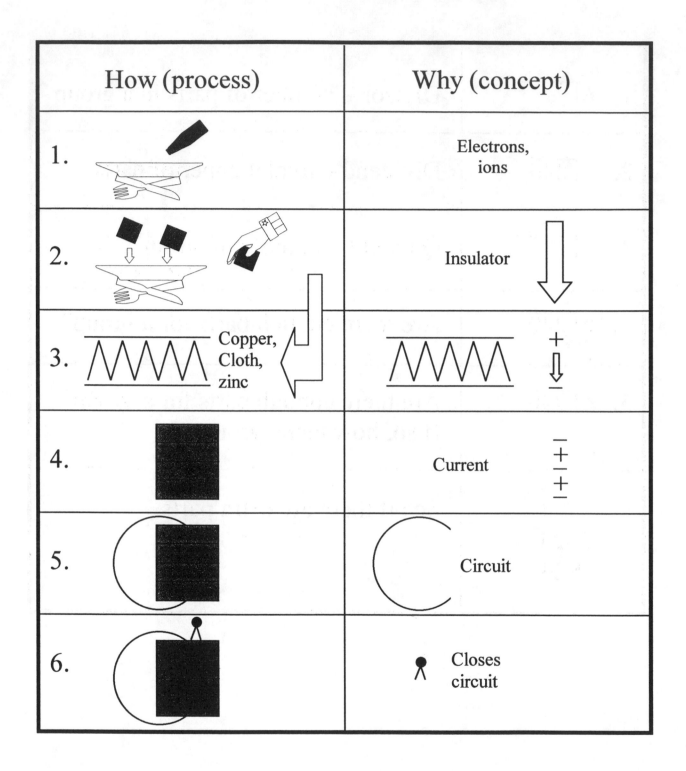	Electrons, ions
2.	Insulator
3. Copper, Cloth, zinc	$+$ $-$
4.	Current
5.	Circuit
6.	Closes circuit

The Little Armored One

The armadillo is a peculiar-looking animal. Its unusual appearance is more like that of a dinosaur than of a mammal living today. In fact, the armadillo is a cousin to some prehistoric animals. However, the armadillo is in little danger of going the way of its extinct relatives. The armadillo population is growing, and the armadillo is actually <u>extending</u> the range of places where it lives. Formerly found mainly in Mexico and South America, this fascinating animal traveled north and east and now lives in Texas, Louisiana, and Oklahoma. Its range is limited only by the frost line, for the armadillo is not suited to cold weather.

The word *armadillo* is Spanish for "little armored one." The animal gets its name from its outer shell. This armored shell is made up of separate plates, which allow the armadillo to curl up into a tight ball and protect its soft underbelly if threatened. This response is a last resort, for the armadillo can usually <u>elude</u> its enemies. It is a very fast runner and strong digger; if it does not outrun its enemies, it can usually burrow to safety.

The little armored one is not a fussy eater. It likes to eat such delicacies as angleworms and cutworms. It has poor vision, so it uses its sharp sense of smell to sniff the bugs out and then digs for them with its nose.

The armadillo's appetite is <u>immense</u>. An armadillo can eat more than 100 cutworms in a single day. Some people believe the effectiveness of the little armored one as a pest controller can outweigh any negative effect its digging may have on garden crops.

One of the most unusual characteristics of the armadillo is the way it crosses water. Since it can hold its breath for as long as six minutes, the armadillo will walk across the bottom of a narrow stream or river. It crosses wider rivers by swallowing air into its stomach and intestines and then floating or paddling across. If the river is moving fast, the little animal will grab hold of pieces of floating wood to help it get to the other side of the river.

The armadillo is harmless and beneficial, interesting and unusual. Some of the characteristics that make it different from other animals have also helped the armadillo to thrive.

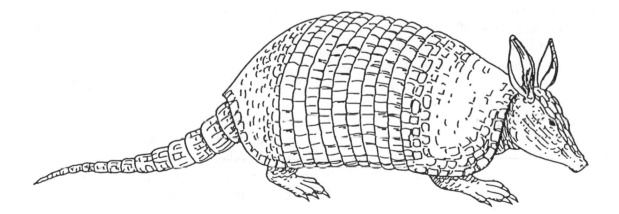

Taken from Texas Assessment of Academic Skills (1996) Grade 5

19. Why might a gardener not want an armadillo in the garden?

    A   An armadillo sometimes damages vegetables as it digs for insects.
    B   An armadillo often attacks gardeners.
    C   An armadillo gives birth in vegetable gardens.
    D   An armadillo attracts bugs that damage garden crops.

20. The word extending in this passage means –

    F   surviving
    G   protecting
    H   restricting
    J   increasing

21. You can tell from the passage that the armadillo –

    A   uses its sharp eyesight to find food
    B   cannot cross large rivers or streams
    C   has been able to adapt to its surroundings
    D   does not have any natural enemies

22. What is the main idea of the second paragraph?

    F   The armadillo's shell is its only protection against enemies.
    G   The armadillo is most often found curled up in a tight ball.
    H   The armadillo has strong claws to dig deep holes.
    J   The armadillo has several ways to protect itself from enemies.

23. According to the passage, it is likely that in the future the armadillo population will –

    A   become extinct
    B   increase in number
    C   move to colder climates
    D   develop soft outer shells

24. In this passage, elude means to –

    F   escape
    G   kill
    H   fight
    J   assist

25. Which is the best summary of this passage?

    A   The armadillo is found mainly in Mexico and South America.
    B   The armadillo has special characteristics that have helped it to survive.
    C   The armadillo has a very unusual diet.
    D   The armadillo is a relative of some prehistoric animals.

26. In this passage, immense means –

    F   ancient
    G   destructive
    H   enormous
    J   wasteful

27. An armadillo swallows air because it –

    A   makes a noise that frightens the armadillo's enemies
    B   lets the armadillo eat less food
    C   increases the armadillo's sense of smell
    D   helps the armadillo to float

Taken from Texas Assessment of Academic Skills (1996) Grade 5

MODULE 15

QUESTION MAKING

QUESTION MAKING

To be able to formulate questions syntactically is very important because without this ability the mind literally can't know what it knows. Many students will ask questions through their voice tone (i.e., You don't have any more????). That is a statement that the voice tone has made into a question. If they cannot examine their own behavior, then the students syntactically or grammatically make it into a question (i.e., Don't you have any more?). Or they ask it in the formal register of their native language.

To do any task, one must be able to go inside the head and ask questions. If individuals cannot, then they can't examine any behavior, nor can they retrieve information in a systematic way. For example, if a teacher says to a student, "Why did you do that?" and the student replies, "I don't know," then the teacher needs to see if the student can ask questions syntactically or in formal register. Chances are very good that the student is saying to himself inside his head, "I did that?"

One of the most important cognitive skills to give to students is having them ask the questions. There are several ways to do this.

1. Playing "Jeopardy!" Jeopardy is when you give the answer, and the student has to come up with the question.

2. Making multiple-choice questions using question stems. Using the question stems on pp. 64-66, have students make their own multiple-choice questions. (Use form on p. 68.)

3. Making question cubes (p. 69).

4. For young students, making them start the first word of a sentence with one of the following words: who, what, when, where, which, how.

5. Reciprocal teaching (p. 63).

6. Using a multiple-choice test, having students tell you why the incorrect answers are wrong. (While this does not give students the ability to ask questions syntactically, it does teach them how to identify wrong answers.)

WHAT IS RECIPROCAL TEACHING?

Reciprocal teaching is the process of asking questions between a teacher and a student. Anne Marie Palinscar found that students who could not ask questions syntactically had significantly lower reading comprehension scores. She also found that they could be taught to ask questions, and this method increased reading achievement.

In reciprocal teaching, these kinds of questions are generated by the student: clarifying, summarizing, and predicting. The student reads a short passage to the teacher. The teacher then asks a question. The student answers. The teacher then reads a short passage to the student. The student generates a question similar to the one the teacher asked. The teacher answers the question.

This is reciprocal teaching.

TAAS Question-Making Stems

1. What does the word _____ mean?
2. What can you tell from the following passage?
3. What does the author give you reason to believe?
4. What is the best summary of this passage?
5. Which of the following is a FACT in this passage?
6. What is the main idea of the _____ paragraph?
7. Which of the following is an opinion in this passage?
8. What happens after _____?
9. How did _____ feel when _____?
10. What is the main idea of this passage?
11. Which of these happened (first/last) in the passage?
12. Which of these is NOT a fact in the passage?
13. Where was _____?
14. When did _____?
15. What happens when _____?
16. What was the main reason for the following _____?
17. After _____, what could _____?
18. Where does the _____ take place?
19. Which of these best describes _____ before/after
    _____?

Taken from Julie Ford

More Question-Making Stems

1. From this passage (story), how might _____ be described?
2. Why was _____?
3. Why did _____?
4. How else might the author have ended the passage (story)?
5. If the author had been _____, how might the information be different?
6. Use the word in a sentence from the passage.) In this passage, what does _____ mean?
7. How did _____ feel about _____?
8. What caused _____ to _____?
9. What is _____?
10. When _____ happened, why did _____?
11. The passage states that _____.
12. Why is that information important to the reader?

Reading-Objective Question Stems

Objective 1: Word Meaning
    In this story the word _____ means …
    The word _____ in this passage means …

Objective 2: Supporting Ideas
    What did _____ do after …?
    What happened just before _____ …?
    What did _____ do first? Last?
    According to the directions given, what was _____ supposed to do first?
       After _____? Last?
    Where does this story take place?
    When does the story take place?

Objective 3: Summarizing Written Texts
    Which sentence tells the main idea of the story?
    This story is mainly about …
    What is the main idea of paragraph 3?
    What is the story mostly about?
    Which statement best summarizes this passage? (paragraph)

Objective 4: Perceiving Relationships and Recognizing Outcomes
    Why did _(name)_ do __(action)___?
    What will happen as a result of _____?
    Based on the information, which is _____ most likely to do?
    What will happen to _____ in this story?
    You can tell from this passage that _____ is most likely to …

Objective 5: Analyzing Information to Make Inference and Generalization
    How did _____ feel about _____?
    How does _____ feel at the beginning (end) of the story?
    According to Figure 1, what …? (Where, how many, when)
    The __(event)___ is being held in order to …
    By __(action)___, __(name)__ was able to show that …
    You can tell from this passage that …?
    Which word best describes _____'s feelings in this passage?

Objective 6: Distinguishing Between Fact and Opinion
    Which of these is a fact expressed in the passage?
    Which of these is an opinion expressed in the passage?

Math Questions

1. Stems need to use the terminology.

2. Distracters are:

   - Incorrect operation

   - Incorrect order

   - Decimal in the wrong place

   - Answer in wrong form (percent instead of number, etc.)

   - Missed step

   - Unnecessary information included

   - Computational errors

Question:

a.

b.

c.

d.

Three Rules:

1. One wrong-answer choice must be funny.

2. Only one answer choice can be right.

3. May not use "all of the above," "none of the above," etc.

Question Cube

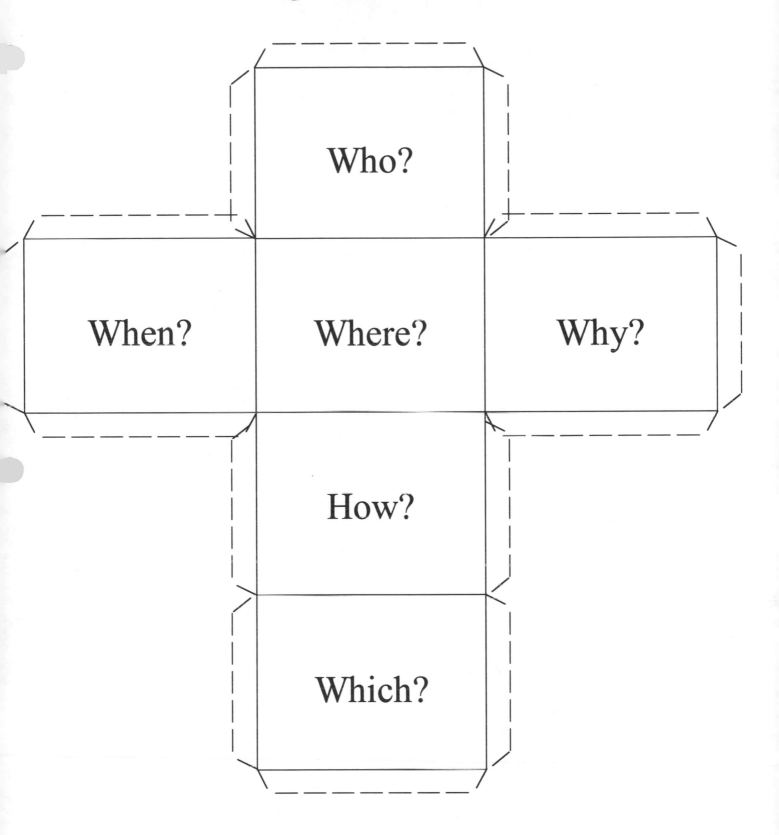

Who?

When? Where? Why?

How?

Which?

MODULE 16

SORTING STRATEGIES THAT USE PATTERNS

SORTING INFORMATION USING PATTERNS AND CRITERIA

To store and retrieve information, one must be able to sort using criteria. However, if the patterns are known, one can sort much faster. Because children from poverty often come into school behind, ways are needed to teach information much faster. Teaching patterns as a way to sort is one way to shorten the time needed to teach something.

The mind sorts data against patterns, mental mindsets, and paradigms to determine what is "important" and what is not.

Items with the same attributes are assigned to a group.

Patterns can be identified using groups.

Abstract constructs are essential for grouping and patterning; these are necessary for success in school.

Here are some ways to teach sorting with the use of criteria and patterns.

1. Sorting M & M's. (Color may not be used as a criterion.)

2. Using patterns to sort text (pp. 77-83).

3. Identifying the criteria used to group or sort (pp. 74-75).

4. Cartooning (p. 76).

Developing Sorting Strategies

The mind sorts data against patterns, mental mindsets, and paradigms to determine what is "important" and what is not.

Attributes become a sort of screen that allows "important" data to continue and stops "unimportant" data.

By teaching patterns within data, students can find what is "important" more quickly and accurately.

Using the column on the left, identify how the examples to the right are alike and different from the column on the left. Circle the words that indicate the way(s) in which the examples to the right are the same.

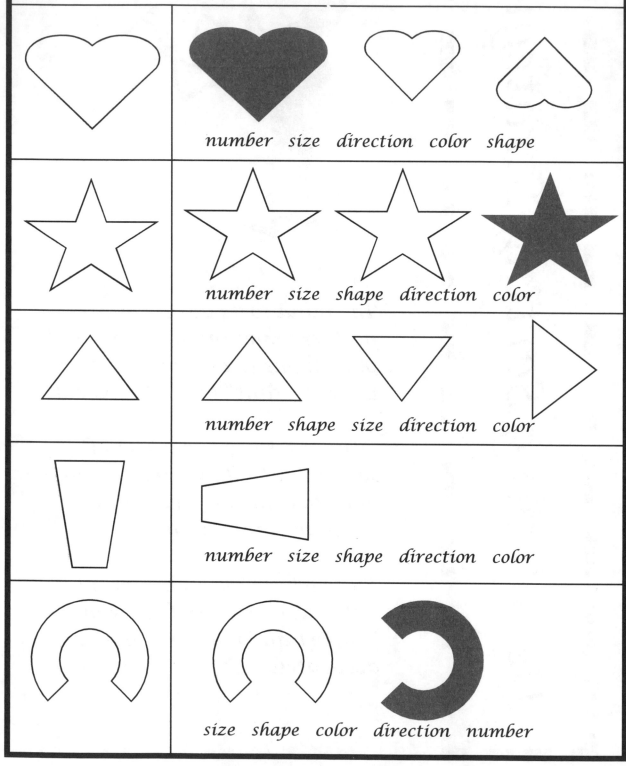

number   size   direction   color   shape

number   size   shape   direction   color

number   shape   size   direction   color

number   size   shape   direction   color

size   shape   color   direction   number

In the first column, write what the words have in common. In the second column, write how the words are different.

Words	Alike	Different
Sugar Salt		
Day Night		
Paper Pencil		
Car Truck		
Now Later		
Here There		
Tall Short		

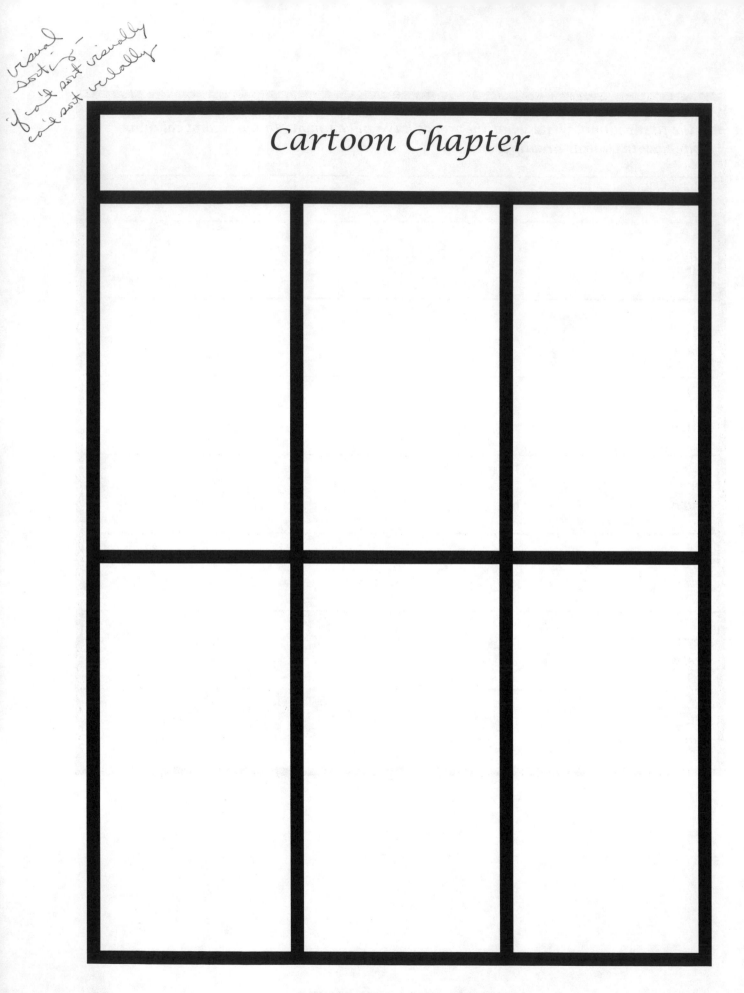

Cartoon Chapter

Sorting Text

Five Common Patterns in Text

purpose of reading or substance of text

	TOPICAL OR DESCRIPTIVE
	SEQUENTIAL narrative, how-to
	FICTION
	TWO SIDES/PARTS cause/effect, pro/con, advantages/ disadvantages
	TAKING A POSITION WITH SUPPORT persuasive, editorial

Five Models to Use
for Sorting

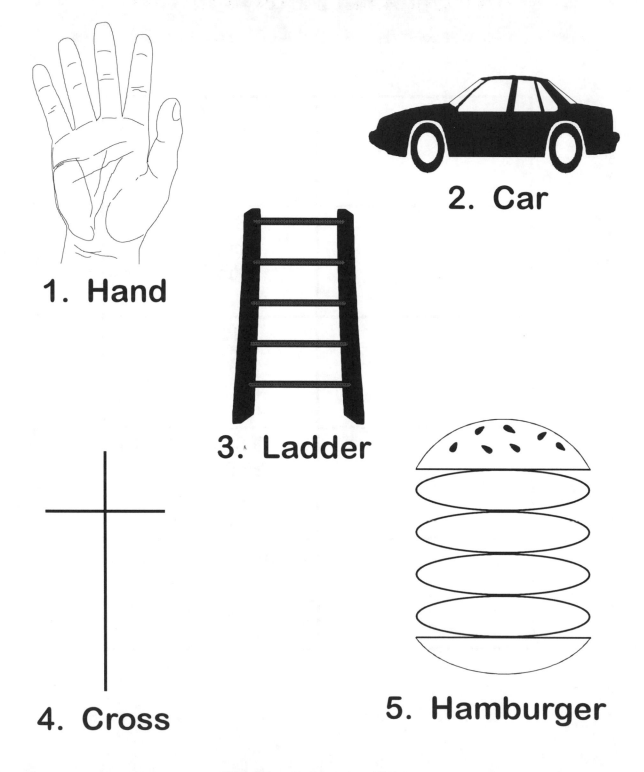

1. Hand

2. Car

3. Ladder

4. Cross

5. Hamburger

Descriptive/Topical

Sequence/How-to

Story Structure

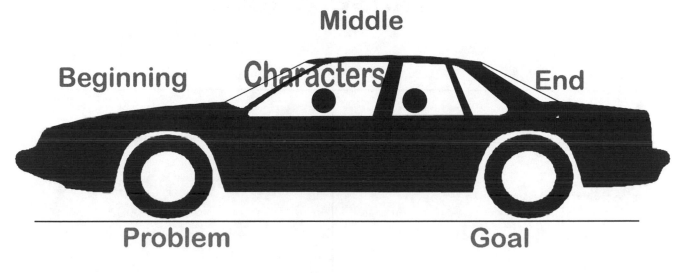

Beginning   Middle   Characters   End

Problem   Goal

Setting

Compare/Contrast
Advantages/Disadvantages
Cause/Effect

Persuasive Reasons

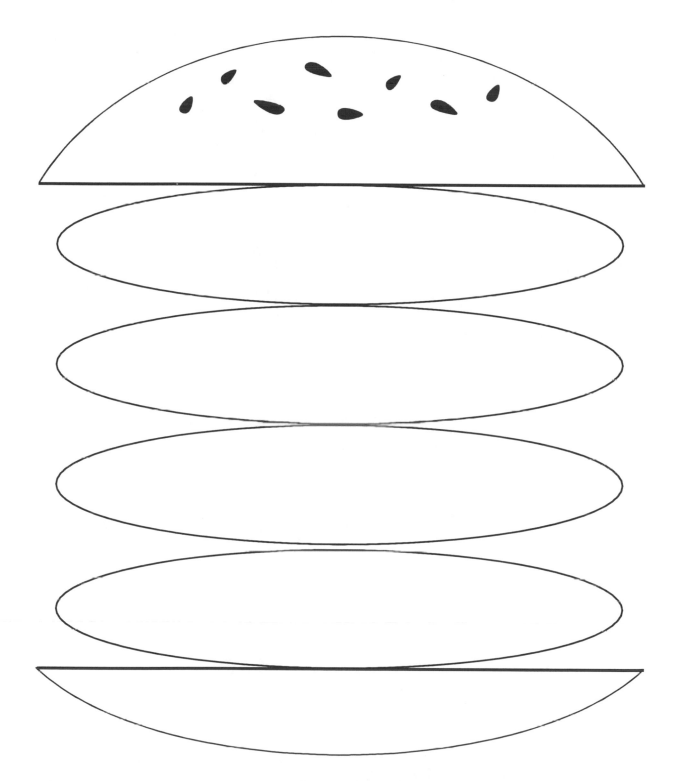

APPENDIX A

Vocabulary Strategies Developed by District 220 Teachers

Barrington, Illinois

The following is a list of strategies suggested by District 220 teachers for implementation of vocabulary development. They have been combined and condensed from suggestions received during the 1991-92 school year. Most are adaptable for use at all grade levels, and all may be altered for personal effectiveness.

Analogies

Students are to determine the relationships between words on a given list and then create their own analogies.

> _Example:_   Bat is to ball as hammer is to nail
> _Materials needed:_   Word list

Bonus Words

Students collect interesting words that they hear throughout the week, write their definitions on cards, and place them in a class "BONUS WORD" box. Teacher draws three words a week; these are displayed around the room as mobiles. The words can be added to spelling lists, used for vocabulary games, or compiled for three to four weeks for a vocabulary challenge.

> _Materials needed:_   Covered shoebox with slit in top, slips of paper

Definition Game

Students as a group define a word. Defined words are collected in a jar. At the end of the period or day, a word is picked from the jar for a student to define. If the definition is correct, the class moves ahead one space on a class game board.

> _Materials needed:_   Vocabulary words and definitions, jar, game board, rewards

Gipe Method

This is recommended for a small number of vocabulary words as a prereading activity.
For example, to teach the word "circulation," the teacher might present the following sentences:

> When the newspaper covered the murder trial, its <u>circulation</u> went up.

> The <u>circulation</u> of a newspaper is how many copies get sold.

> If you owned a newspaper and the <u>circulation</u> was going down, what would you do?

> _Materials needed:_   Vocabulary words and teacher-prepared sentence, definition,
>   and question for each one

Individual Word Banks

Students collect words that they find unique or interesting. These words can be compiled in at least three ways:

      A. Individual word journal
      B. Index cards strung on a ring
      C. Displayed as a mobile

      Materials needed: Journal or index cards and ring

Word Illustrations

From a list of words, students choose one to define and illustrate. One way of implementing this would be to take a 4-by-6 index card and fold in half (width-wise). The word is written on the outside. When the card is opened, the definition is on the top half of the card, with the illustration on the bottom half of the card. Using sticky-tac, the cards are then affixed to a wall or displayed on a bulletin board.

Word illustrations are fast and simple to use; at the same time they have the benefit of solidifying concepts.

Knowledge Ratings

Using a graph like the one below, students list the words to be studied in the first column. They evaluate their knowledge level of each word and check the appropriate box. If they have some idea of the meaning, they write in their guess. Following discussion or study, they write the definition in their own words. This actiivity is particularly useful in helping students develop metacogntive awareness.

	Know	Think I know	Have heard		
Word				**Guess**	**Definition**
saline			x	a liquid for contact lenses	a salt solution

Acting It Out

The possibilities are limitless. An activity can be as simple as a student ambling across the room to dramatize the word "amble." Following are a few other possibilities:

- While the teacher is reading a passage, students take on character roles.
- Students accompany a reading with appropriate sound effects.
- Students use props and simple costumes to dramatize the retelling of a story.
- Students pantomime a particular word.

Dramatization is especially engaging to students. Sensorimotor involvement enhances retention of concepts.

Word Dangles

Students read a novel or story and then, on a piece of construction paper, illustrate it and write a summary of it. From the selection, they choose approximately five words that interest them, then write and illustrate each word on a separate card. They write a definition of the word on the reverse side of the card. The cards subsequently are attached to the bottom of the construction paper and "dangle" from it. The finished product can be hung as a mobile.

By using "word dangles," students enhance their comprehension. The illustrations also help them with conceptualization. They learn how vocabulary, reading, and writing are connected. The strategy is adaptable for all content arms, including fine arts. For example, in math, students might write a summary of a process and write, define, and illustrate several key words for that process. "Word dangles" also provide a word-rich environment and stimulate student interest in vocabulary study.

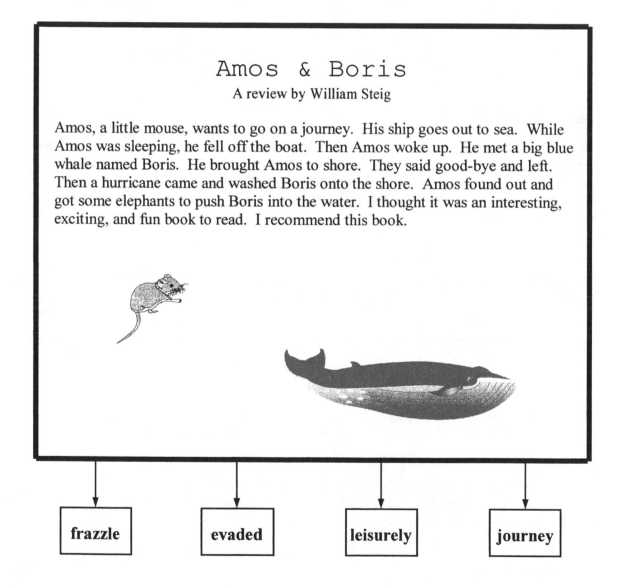

Amos & Boris

A review by William Steig

Amos, a little mouse, wants to go on a journey. His ship goes out to sea. While Amos was sleeping, he fell off the boat. Then Amos woke up. He met a big blue whale named Boris. He brought Amos to shore. They said good-bye and left. Then a hurricane came and washed Boris onto the shore. Amos found out and got some elephants to push Boris into the water. I thought it was an interesting, exciting, and fun book to read. I recommend this book.

| frazzle | evaded | leisurely | journey |

Word Walls

Each letter of the alphabet gets a space on the wall. Both the teacher and students suggest words. Students place their choices on an "add" list, and the teacher discusses the choices with students before making the final selection. Words are then posted on the word wall according to the first letter of the word. Choices are flexible. They can be words students want to know more about, words of general interest, words taken from readings, and special-category words. The word wall may stay up all year, but the actual words placed on the wall will vary according to need and interest.

Word walls are particularly flexible. For example, they can be used with a literature unit, a study of word deviations, or structural analysis or a social studies unit. Furthermore, all teachers, both classroom and special-area, can use such walls to enhance curriculum. One additional advantage is the minimal teacher preparation required. Finally, word walls provide a word-rich environment and stimulate student interest in vocabulary study.

A	B	C
adrift	bail	cruise
D	**E**	**F**
driftwood	evaded	frazzle

Picture It

With each new story/reading, assign each student one vocabulary word. Students must:

- find the word in the story/reading and record the page number (see form below)
- find the word in the dictionary and record the pronunciation, number of syllables, part of speech, and definition used in the story
- create a picture the word (on back of form below) to represent the word
- present the word to the class using the picture and definition

Example:

```
_____      _____
        (word)                (page number)

_____  _____  _____
(pronunciation) (# of syllables)  (part of speech)

Definition from story_____

_____
```

Intermediate Adaptation

With each text reading, assign each student one vocabulary word. Students must:

- find the word in text
- copy text definition (taken directly from book)
- write own definition (in student's own words)
- use discriminating/distinguishing characteristics (information that helps to give more details about the word)
- draw illustration (drawing that gives a visual representation of the word)

Example:

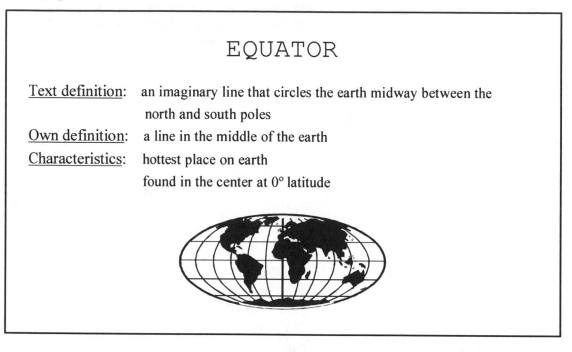

EQUATOR

Text definition: an imaginary line that circles the earth midway between the
                         north and south poles

Own definition: a line in the middle of the earth

Characteristics: hottest place on earth
                         found in the center at 0° latitude

Materials needed: Text reading, vocabulary list, teacher-developed worksheet

M-R-M (Match-Read-Match)

- Students are given X number of vocabulary words from a certain chapter or article and xnumber of definitions. All are cut into 2-by-4 pieces and mixed up.
- Students match words with meaning before reading.
- Students read to find meanings.
- Students match words and definitions. The page number on which the word was found must be indicated on the card.
- Oral discussion.

Materials needed: Vocabulary words, reading material, and vocabulary/
                         definition cards

Semantic-Feature Analysis

This two-dimensional matrix integrates new information with familiar information, develops knowledge of relationships, and establishes connections. It works best using words that are closely related, with some words familiar to students. The vocabulary words are listed in the first column, and the semantic features are listed on the first row.

Semantic Feature Analysis

	flies	has four legs	lives in water
bird	+	-	-
dog	-	+	-
cat	-	+	-
penguin	0	-	-

+ = yes
- = no
0 = does not apply, or both yes and no

Materials needed: Vocabulary list, semantic-feature chart

Spell the Word

Students are divided into groups of two, three, or four. Each group of students is given a set of letters. In the set are three of each of the most commonly used letters in the alphabet (*a, e, i, o, u, m, p, r, s, t*). There are two of each of the other letters of the alphabet in the set. Members of each group then place the alphabet in front of them.

A definition of a word is read, and each group must correctly spell the word that matches the definition. A point is given to the first team that correctly spells the correct word.

Synonyms

Provide a bulletin board or classroom door on which synonyms for overly used words such as "said" or "nice" can be displayed. This can be a yearlong display and used as a writing resource.

Materials needed: Bulletin board, classroom door or wall, cards on which to write synonyms

Word Web

Students write the target word in the box and then write a synonym, an antonym, a definition, and an experience to complete the web.

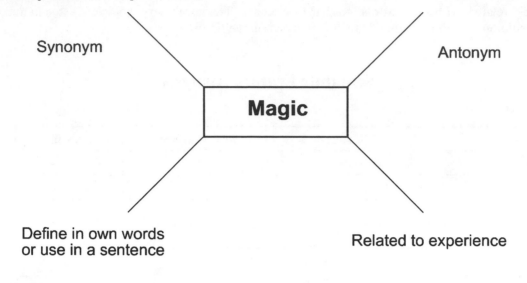

Synonym

Antonym

Magic

Define in own words
or use in a sentence

Related to experience

Word Art

Students brainstorm a list of words relating to a particular subject (i.e., winter, Halloween, geometry). Using these words, students then design an object related to the subject, such as a ghost shape using Halloween words.

Materials needed: Brainstormed word list, paper, colored pencils or markers

Word Collector

Students are informed that they are word collectors. Their assignment is to find as many words as they can in their resource materials, textbook, newspapers, magazines, etc., to fit into categories designed for the subject.

Example: In a desert unit, words may be categorized as follows:

    A. Names of deserts
    B. Living things in desert
    C. Desert terrain

Students categorize words by writing them in the proper columns as the words are found. Students then discuss their findings, and new terms are added to their lists and explained.

Materials needed: Reading material, word-collector chart

A. Names of deserts	B. Living things in desert	C. Desert terrain
Mojave	Cactus	Dunes

Word of the Month

Students brainstorm "words of the month" for a class chart. New words can continually be added throughout the month. These words can be used for categorizing activities – as a writing resource or as bonus spelling words.

>_Materials Needed:_   Brainstormed word list on a class chart

Parent Project

Each week, two weeks, or month, parents read a story or stories with their children. Children are to choose x number of "interesting words" from the material to read at home. These interesting words can be compiled on a class chart and used for vocabulary development or for creative-writing projects.

>_Materials needed:_   Letter to parents explaining project, class chart

Jigsaw

Students are placed in cooperative groups. Each group is presented with the same set of vocabulary words, and each student in a group gets one of them. Students then regroup according to the word they have, and the new groups decide on an appropriate definition for their word. Students then return to their original group, and each child teaches his/her word to the other students in that group.

>_Materials needed:_   Vocabulary words

Venn Diagrams

Students work in cooperative groups brainstorming homophones and writing them in sentences. The groups share their lists/sentences, and the words are put on a homophone bulletin board. Because students are using a dictionary to check spelling and meaning, they discover many words that have multiple meanings but are not homophones. This leads to a Venn diagram showing/   comparing multiple-meaning words and homophones.

Jeopardy!

Make a Jeopardy! board. Put vocabulary words on cards to stick in each pocket. Have the students come up at random and select a card. The word should not be showing. Have the students use the word in a sentence and give a definition for it. The class can earn popcorn kernels for each right definition. In the sample on p. 94, students would earn 10 kernels for a word in the top row, 20 kernels for a word in the middle row, and 30 kernels for a word in the bottom row. Put the kernels that students earn into a jar. When the jar is full, the class has a popcorn party.

Sample Jeopardy Board

10	10	10	10
20	20	20	20
30	30	30	30

Materials needed: Jeopardy board, vocabulary words on cards, popcorn kernels, jars

Ladder

Students use related words to design word ladders. The closer the words on the ladder, the more synonymous they are in meaning.

Example:

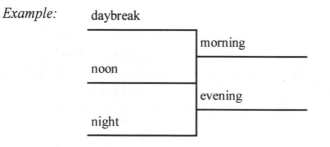

Materials needed: Word groups, ladder format

Log Sheet

Using a list of words, the teacher develops the following format:

Patrol   _____ * patrol _____ : to guard by walking around.

* The police officer patrolled the neighborhood.*

Why would you have to patrol a building? * _____

_____

* Student-completed portions

Materials needed: Vocabulary list, teacher-developed worksheet

Word Sort

A word sort is a way to increase word recognition and develop vocabulary meaning.

Begin with a word list. The list may be student- or teacher-generated. Words may be from new or old materials. For older students, you may want to use words from content-area materials.

Pass out to each student, or pair of students, a set of your words. Students need to sort the words by the similarities and differences they see. (All words should be read aloud prior to sorting.) After the words have been put into categories, the students explain their reasons for their categories.

Suggested categories might include:

• alphabetical order

• word length

• spelling features (same ending, beginning, etc.)

• words familiar to them/unfamiliar to them

• common consonants/vowels

• words inside of words

• compound words

• base words

• parts of speech

Using word sorts as a learning method gives students the advantage of the tactile sense. Saying the words and explaining the rationale develop language communication. Seeing the way one word may fit into a variety of groups not only provides reinforcement of quick sight recall of the word but also extends understanding that one word may have multiple meanings in different contexts.

Using word sorts allows the student to see words as a whole and also to distinguish the small parts that make words different. Word sorts let the student see how words fit together and how they stand alone.

Predictogram

Predict how the author will use these words in the story to tell about:

The Setting	The Characters	The Problem
The Action	The Resolution	Other Things

Using a Picture Dictionary to Build Sight Vocabulary

A large sight vocabulary enables a student to read fluently and focus attention on making sense of a passage. A "Pictionary" helps to build a "real word" sight vocabulary, not an abstract vocabulary. Words are the verbal labels for concepts.

Possible steps to develop a picture vocabulary:

1. Show a picture that includes many or all of the new vocabulary (i.e., a park or a winter scene).

2. Go over the picture, highlighting the target words that are to be taught.

3. Go over specific words and spellings. Say the word, spell the word, say the word.

4. Locate the vocabulary words in the Pictionary.

5. Individually, if possible, have the students spell the word to you when they have found it.

6. Have the students draw or cut and paste pictures of the given word(s).

7. Students should show their completed work to the teacher. Students may use the "buddy system" to check each other's work.

Reinforcing activities:

1. Words from Pictionary units may be used for "word bingo."

2. Concentration – match words and pictures.

3. Classify words, using learned Pictionary vocabulary.

4. Have students look up completed Pictionary words in their "Pictionary dictionary" for practice.

Developing Vocabulary Activities

Concept Building

1. Guessing Opposites or Seeing Relationships

To a small group, the teacher says:

> Candy is sweet, but pickles are _____
> An airplane is fast, but a horse is _____
> The sky is above; the ground is _____

This type of procedure can also be used to elicit relationships.

Example:

> Pies are made by a baker; clothes are made by a _____
> A cat runs on its legs, but a car runs on _____
> In the morning the sun rises; at night the sun _____

The level at which this exercise can be done will vary widely with different children.

2. Concepts Related to Word Perception

When children begin to read from charts, trade books, and pre-primers, they must distinguish between words that look somewhat alike. To do this they must be able to understand and use such concepts as:

> same/different
> smaller/larger
> big/bigger/biggest
> up/down
> tall/short
> right/left

Most of these can be contributing to a focal idea. Games are good; for example, to develop correct ideas of up and down, the children may play the game "Simon says, 'Thumbs up,' 'thumbs down.'"

You may dramatize or give directions as they say the nursery rhyme "Jack and Jill." Other games may be devised for tall and short, as well as other concepts.

3. Storytelling: Round Robin

The children sit around in a circle. The teacher starts off by saying, "Once there was a little boy." Individual children are called on, each to make up a sentence until a story is completed.

4. Storytelling: Picture Covers

Covers of new and old juvenile storybooks may be used for this game. The covers may be those of familiar stories or new stories. The children sit in a circle, the teacher holds up a cover, and the children "guess" what the story is about. If it is new, they tell a story; if it is a familiar one, they try to retell the story. Several children are called on to get a variety of stories and ideas. Picture postcards, magazine pictures, and travel pictures may all be used if old covers are not available.

5. Wall Charts

A large wall chart with pictures of all the characters in a story is made. In the left margin the teacher prints a word that goes with the story. For example, the word "mother" accompanies the familiar picture associated with the mother in a particular story. After the children are acquainted with the words and pictures, a "window show" can be given. In one end of a large carton or shoebox is cut a square big enough to show the larger picture. A piece of cellophane pasted over the square will give it a window-like effect. The teacher or child places one of the familiar chart pictures in the window, and a child points to the word on the wall chart that belongs with that picture. For variation, the word may be exposed in the window and the picture pointed to on the chart. Children don't have to read words at this stage; this type of general identification is   sufficient.

6. Experience Charts

Whenever the opportunity arises, children should be encouraged to write stories as a group. These stories can later be bound and made available to the group so they can look at and talk about them. The stories that grow out of natural activities, special events, trips, and discussions can be used for the experience charts. The vocabulary level is of relatively little importance at the readiness level since the charts are not so much for exact reading of details as for providing broadening experiences and developing interest in reading. A pet brought to school often creates a good deal of interest. In such an event, a story about it can be written. For example:

>We have a turtle.
>His name is Pokey.
>Pokey is very slow.
>Pokey lives in water.
>Pokey plays in water.

As children become acquainted with the use of experience charts, they may begin to pick out a familiar word or two. Gradually, more emphasis can be given to sight vocabulary, but this occurs as children enter the beginning reading stage.

7. Directions Game

To build concepts of direction, play the directions game. A child is called to the front of the room and given three simple directions to carry out. For example, the teacher says, "Go to the back of the room, touch the easel, then hop back to the front of the room."

APPENDIX B

Improving Test Scores and Student Achievement

QUARTILE	NATIVE AMERICAN	HISPANIC	AFRICAN AMERICAN	ASIAN	CAUCASIAN	LOW SOCIOECONOMIC STATUS

Tracking student progress by quartile helps measure student growth and determine the amount of progress that is probable in a given year.

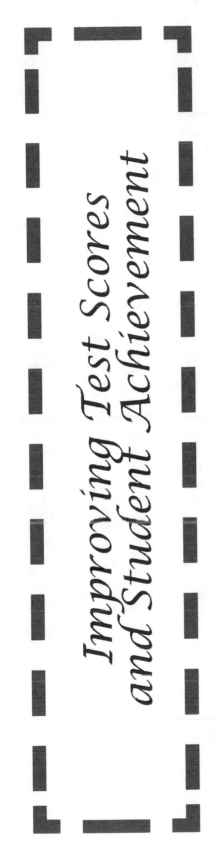

Improving Test Scores and Student Achievement

Four Factors That Make a Difference in Learning and Student Achievement

1. Amount of time

2. Clarity of the focus of instruction

3. What the student came in knowing

4. Interventions of the teacher

CAMPUSWIDE INTERVENTIONS THAT
IMPROVE STUDENT ACHIEVEMENT

by Ruby K. Payne, Ph.D.
Educational Consultant

'With simpler models of staff development that are operational and involve 100% of the staff, the roller-coaster ride that students take through school can be smoothed out significantly.'

Conversation between a principal new to the building and a supervisor:

Supervisor: "This campus cannot be low-performing again. I do not have any extra money to give you. With the Title I money you have at your campus, your school will need to find a way to raise your achievement significantly."

Principal (to herself as she walks to the car): "And just how is this to happen? I have 1,100 students, 80% low-income, 12 new teachers, a mobility rate of 40%. I know it can be done, but in a year?"

Many of our models for staff development and curriculum development do not address realities pressuring schools today. Some of these realities are:

~ The critical mass needed to impact student achievement. Example: Ninety percent of teachers are not doing a particular intervention or strategy versus 10% doing it.
~ The growing knowledge base required of teachers and administrators. Example: Educators are to know about sexual harassment, inclusion, cooperative learning, reading strategies, ADHD, modifications, gifted/talented strategies, legal guidelines, ESL strategies, etc.
~ The time frames in which student achievement is to occur and be measured. Example: State and norm-referenced tests are designed for annual measures of learning.
~ The accountability criteria that schools must meet. Example: In Texas, Academic Excellence Indicator System data and Texas Assessment of Academic Skills data are used to determine accreditation status.
~ The lack of money and time for extensive training for teachers. Example: Most districts and campuses have five days or less of staff development, which limits the length and/or depth of the training.
~ The increased number of students who come from poverty and/or who lack support systems at home. Example: When the school system does not address their children's needs, educated parents tend to provide assistance, pay for a tutor, or request a teacher. In poverty, usually the only interventions a student receives are through school.
~ The growing number of new teachers spurred by the surge in the school-age population. Example: The school-age population in America is expected to increase 25% by 2010.

Processes and models are available to address these needs. But to do so, an additional model for staff development and curriculum development must be used. This model basically trades in-depth learning for critical mass by using a simpler approach. Michael Fullan talks about the importance of critical mass, as well as the main criteria teachers use to determine how "user friendly" the curriculum and training are, i.e., how operational they are (Fullan, 1991; Fullan, 1996)

In these models, which I have used for several years, the amount of time spent in training is decreased, the model is less complex and totally operational, and 100% of the staff is trained. We still will need reflective staff development; we just need an additional model to help address some of the aforementioned issues.

Figure A

Factors Affecting Staff Development	Reflective Staff Development	Operational Staff Development
Definition	Process by which individual examines in-depth his/her learning on given subject	Method for immediate implementation across system to address accountability and student achievement
Purpose	To build in-depth learning and change	To impact system quickly; to build in connections/linkages across system
Effect on critical mass	Depends on amount of resources and level of attrition; takes at least four to five years	Affects critical mass almost immediately; can have 80% to 90% implementation first year
Time required	Four to five days per person for initial training	Two hours to one day of training per person
Breadth	Limited	Systemic
Cost analysis	High per-person cost	Low per-person cost
District role	May be contracted or may use district expertise to deliver and provide follow-up	Identifies with campuses' systemic needs to be addressed; works with campuses to reach critical mass; assists with operational development of innovation
Follow-up	Provided in small groups or by expert trainer	Provided through accountability measures and fine-tuning from discussions to make innovation more user-friendly
Role of principal	Is liaison with training; may provide resources and follow-up opportunities	Assists with delivery of training; provides insistence, expectations, and support for innovation

What does this information mean in practice? With simpler models that are operational and involve 100% of the staff, the roller-coaster ride that students take through school can be smoothed out significantly. One of the reasons that most middle-class students do better in school is that their parents intervene to lessen the impact of the roller coaster. (These parents do so by paying for tutoring, requesting teachers, and providing assistance and instruction at home.)

Figure B

Johnny's Progress	Grade 1	Grade 2	Grade 3	Grade 4	Grade 5
Grade 1	X				
Grade 2	X				
Grade 3		X			
Grade 4		X			
Grade 5					

As you can see in Figure B, the X represents Johnny and his journey through five years of school. In first grade, he had a wonderful teacher who willingly went to every kind of training available. Johnny had a great year and made the expected progress.

In second grade, his teacher was having many health problems and missed quite a few days of school. In addition, Johnny's parents divorced, so he was shuttled between homes. In second grade, Johnny actually regressed.

In third grade, Johnny had a beginning teacher. She loved the students but did not have the experience or the guidelines to provide the instruction the other third-grade teacher did. Most of the educated parents had asked for the other teacher because of her excellent reputation. Johnny made little progress.

In fourth grade, Johnny had a teacher who did not participate in staff development. As far as she was concerned, it was a waste of time. Her students tended to do poorly on the state test, but her husband was on the school board. Once again, given her reputation, the educated parents had requested that their children be placed in the other fourth-grade classroom.

In fifth grade, it was determined that Johnny was now 2½ grade levels behind and should possibly be tested for Special Education.

How can we address this problem? With systemic interventions that can impact achievement through simple yet effective tools and processes.

Benjamin Bloom (1976) did extensive research to determine what makes a difference in learning. He identified four factors: (1) the amount of time to learn, (2) the intervention(s) of the teacher, (3) how clear the focus of the instruction is, and (4) what the student came in knowing. As is readily apparent, the control the individual teacher has over these variables is significantly impacted by what is happening at the school. When these interventions are addressed on a campuswide level in a systematic way, more learning occurs.

Systemic interventions that can impact achievement are:

1. *Reasonable expectations.* This is a simple model of curriculum mapping that addresses the focus of instruction and the amount of time.
2. *Growth assessments.* These are methods for identifying and assessing on a regular basis the growth a student makes.
3. *Benchmarks.* This is a relatively simple model of three to four indicators by grading period to show whether a student needs an immediate intervention. *It is absolutely crucial for first-grade reading.* Research indicates that a first-grader who isn't in the primer by April of the first-grade year generally doesn't progress beyond the third-grade reading level.
4. *Interventions for the student.* When students are identified through the growth assessments and benchmarks as making inadequate growth, immediate interventions are provided for the student, one of which is allowing more time during the school day.

What follows are a description and example for each of the above. *It is important to note that all of these are working documents of one or two pages so that they can constantly be reassessed.* It is analogous to having a road map: Not all of the details are present. However, the "lay of the land," the choices of route, and the final destination are clear.

Reasonable Expectations

Reasonable expectations identify what is taught and the amount of time devoted to it. This allows a campus to "data mine," i.e., determine the payoff between what actually gets taught, the amount of time given to it, and the corresponding test results. For example, if two hours a day are spent on reading, but only 15 minutes are devoted to students actually reading, the payoff will be less than if 45 minutes of that time are devoted to students actually reading.

Figure C (see next page) is the process used. For each subject area, it requires about 30 to 60 minutes of individual time, one to two hours of grade-level time, and three hours of total faculty time.

Figure D (see pp. 141-142) is an example from Runyan Elementary in Conroe, Texas. The principal is Nancy Harris.

Figure C

One of the first pieces of information that a principal and campus need to know is *what is actually being taught.* Here's a simple process to help find this out:

1. If you are on a six-weeks grading period, divide a paper into six equal pieces. If you are on a nine-weeks grading period, divide a paper into four equal pieces. Have each teacher for each subject area write the units or skills that he/she teaches in each grading period. In other words, what does the teacher usually manage to teach to that grade level in that subject area in that amount of time?

2. Have each grade level meet and discuss one subject area at a time. Do all the teachers at a grade level basically have the same expectations for that grade level in terms of content and skills? Have they come to a consensus about the expectations for that grade level?

3. Have the faculty as a group compare the grade levels 1 through 5, 6 through 8, or 9 through 12. If Johnny was with the school for five years, what would he have the opportunity to learn? What would he not have had the opportunity to learn? Where are the holes in the opportunities to learn?

4. The faculty then uses this information to identify the strengths and weaknesses in the current educational program. Are some things repeated without benefit to achievement? Are some things not ever taught or so lightly brushed over so as not to be of benefit? What is included that could be traded out for something that has a higher payoff in achievement?

5. When the discussion is over, the one-page sheets are revised and given to the appropriate teachers.

6. Twice a year, the principal meets with grade-level teams and, using these sheets, discusses the progress of the learning, adjustments that need to be made, etc. These become working documents and, because of their simplicity, they can easily be revised.

Figure D

Second-Grade Language Arts Curriculum *(70% fiction, 30% non-fiction)*	
First six weeks	**Second six weeks**
Reading – 60 minutes DEAR (Drop Everything and Read) – 10 minutes Teacher reading to students Reading workshop – 50 minutes	*Reading – 60 minutes* DEAR – 10 minutes Teacher reading to students Reading workshop – 50 minutes
Spelling – 15 minutes, 60 words total 10 *words/week*	*Spelling – 15 minutes, 60 words total* 10 *words/week*
Writing – 45 minutes Personal narrative, two to three sentences, same subject DOL (Daily Oral Language) – 15 minutes Writing workshop – 30 minutes	*Writing – 45 minutes* Six to seven lines on same subject for how-to DOL – 15 minutes Writing workshop – 30 minutes
Vocabulary (integrated) – five words/week	*Vocabulary (integrated) – five words/week*
Skills – 20 minutes Choosing a just-right book Characters Predicting Distinguishing between fiction and non- fiction	*Skills – 20 minutes* Setting Beginning, middle, end of story Parts of speech: noun, verb Sequential order Comprehension Compound words Contractions

Third six weeks	**Fourth six weeks**
Reading – 60 minutes DEAR – 10 minutes Teacher reading to students Reading workshop – 50 minutes	*Reading – 60 minutes* DEAR – 15 minutes Teacher reading to students Reading workshop – 45 minutes
Spelling – 15 minutes, 60 words total 10 *words/week*	*Spelling – 15 minutes, 60 words total* 10 *words/week* ABC order to second letter

Writing – 45 minutes
Five to seven steps in paragraph form,
    sequential for how-to
DOL – 15 minutes
	Writing – 45 minutes
	How-to: five to seven steps in paragraph form
	DOL – 15 minutes, TAAS (Texas Assessment
	    of Academic Skills) form

Third six weeks (continued)	Fourth six weeks (continued)
Writing workshop – 30 minutes *Vocabulary (integrated) – five words/week* *Skills – 20 minutes* Main idea Prefixes, suffixes Context clues Synonyms, antonyms, homophones, homonyms Comprehension Compound words Contractions	Writing workshop – 30 minutes *Vocabulary (integrated) – five words/week* *Skills – 20 minutes* Quotes Draw conclusions Make inferences Adjectives/adverbs Comprehension Possessives Compound words Contractions

Fifth six weeks	Sixth six weeks
Reading – 60 minutes DEAR – 15 minutes Teacher reading to students Reading workshop – 45 minutes *Spelling – 15 minutes, 60 words total* 10 *words/week* ABC order to second letter *Writing – 45 minutes* Descriptive writing – seven sentences Compare/contrast DOL – 15 minutes, TAAS form Writing workshop – 30 minutes *Vocabulary (integrated) – five words/ week* *Skills – 20 minutes* Main idea distinguished from details Fact/opinion Cause/effect Comprehension Possessives Compound words Contractions	*Reading 60 minutes* DEAR – 15 minutes Teacher reading to students Reading workshop – 45 minutes *Spelling – 15 minutes, 60 words total* 10 *words/week* ABC order to third letter *Writing – 45 minutes* Summary Compare/contrast DOL – 15 minutes, TAAS form Writing workshop – 30 minutes *Vocabulary (integrated) – five words/week* *Skills – 20 minutes* Recognize propaganda and point of view Comprehension Possessives Compound words Contractions

Growth Assessments

Any number of growth assessments are available. What makes something a growth assessment is that it identifies movement against a constant set of criteria. What makes a growth assessment different from a test is that the criteria do not change in a growth assessment. Rubrics are one way to measure and identify growth.

Figure E (see next page) is an example of a reading rubric to measure student growth. It was developed by Sandra Duree, Karen Coffey, and me in conjunction with the teachers of Goose Creek Consolidated Independent School District, Baytown, Texas. *Becoming a Nation of Readers* identifies characteristics of skilled readers, so those characteristics were used to measure growth as a constant over five years. We identify what growth would look like over five years if a student were progressing as a skilled reader.

To develop a growth assessment, a very simple process can be used. Have the teachers in your building (who consistently get the highest achievement and who understand the district curriculum and statewide educational specs) develop the growth assessment. Keep in mind these guidelines: (1) The purpose is to identify the desired level of achievement, (2) the growth assessment needs to be simple and easily understood, and (3) student movement or growth toward the desired level of achievement must be clear.

Here are the steps for creating a growth assessment:

1. Identify three to five criteria.
2. Set up a grid with numerical values (1 through 4 is usually enough).
3. Identify what would be an excellent piece of work or demonstration. That becomes #4.
4. Work backwards: Next identify what would be a 3 and so on.

When the growth assessment is developed, it needs to go back to the faculty for feedback and refinement. When there is substantial agreement and at least 80% buy-in, the faculty needs to move forward with it.

Figure E

Reading Rubric, Grade 1			

Student name: _____ School year: _____

Campus: _____ Grade: _____

	Beginning	Developing	Capable	Expert
Fluency	Decodes words haltingly	Decodes sentences haltingly	Knows vowel teams (ea, ee, oa, etc.)	Decodes polysyllabic words
	Misses key sounds	Knows conditions for long vowels (vowel at end of syllable, e.g., me, he)	Identifies common spelling patterns	Decodes words in context of paragraphs
	Identifies most letter sounds	Identifies blends and consonants	Uses word-attack skills to identify new words	Decodes words accurately and automatically
	Identifies short vowels	Decodes diagraphs and r-control vowels (or, ar, er, etc.)	Reads sentences in meaningful sequence	Reads paragraphs in meaningful sequence
	Says/recognizes individual words	Reads at rate that doesn't interfere with meaning	Reads with expression	Reads with expression, fluency, appropriate tone, and pronunciation
Constructive	Predictions are incomplete, partial, and unrelated	Predicts what might happen next	Predicts story based upon pictures and other clues	Can predict possible endings to story with some accuracy
	Predictions indicate no or inappropriate prior knowledge	Makes minimal links to personal experience/prior knowledge	Relates story to personal experience/prior knowledge	Can compare/contrast story with personal experience
Motivated	Does not read independently	Reads when teacher or parent requests	Will read for specific purpose	Initiates reading on own
	Concentrates on decoding	Is eager to use acquired skills (words and phrases)	Uses new skills frequently in self-selected reading	Reads for pleasure
Strategic	Does not self-correct	Recognizes mistakes but has difficulty in self-correcting	Has strategies for self-correction (reread, read ahead, ask questions, etc.)	Analyzes self-correction strategies as to best strategy
	Is uncertain as to how parts of story fit together	Can identify characters and setting in story	Can identify characters, setting, and events of story	Can talk about story in terms of problem and/or goal

Process	Cannot tell what has been read	Does not sort important from unimportant	Can determine with assistance what is important and unimportant	Organizes reading by sorting important from unimportant

Benchmarks

Figure F (see next page) is one example. As you can see from the example, benchmarks are very simple. They identify the critical attributes that students must acquire each six weeks if they are to progress. If the student has not demonstrated these benchmarks, then immediate additional interventions must begin.

How does one get benchmarks? Once again, identify the experienced educators who always have high student achievement. Ask them how they know a student will have trouble. They already know the criteria. And by putting it in writing and having a common understanding, teachers, particularly those who are new to teaching or who are not as experienced, can more readily make interventions and address student progress. It then needs to go back to the grade level for their feedback and changes.

Figure F

Benchmarks for Fourth-grade Language Arts

If a student cannot do the following, then immediate interventions need to be made.

First six weeks
- Edit fragments and run-ons in own writing.
- Identify and define figurative and literal meaning.
- Write elaborated, organized descriptive paper.
- Be able to choose just-right books.

Second six weeks
- Identify story structure orally and in written form.
- Write organized, elaborated expressive narrative.
- Identify correct subject/verb agreement and use in everyday writing.
- Use correct pronoun forms in everyday writing.

Third six weeks
- Read passage and use contextual clues to decode unknown words.
- Read passage and recall facts and details orally and in writing.
- Read story or paragraph and sequence major events.
- Write organized, elaborated how-to.

Fourth six weeks
- Read passage and identify main idea, orally and in written summary.
- Read passage and paraphrase orally and in writing.
- Write organized, elaborated classificatory paper.
- Read passage and identify best summary.
- Write three- to four-sentence paragraph.

Fifth six weeks
- Use graphic sources to answer questions.
- Read passage, then predict outcomes and draw conclusions.
- Distinguish between fact and non-fact, between stated and non-stated opinion.
- After reading passage, be able to tell cause of event or effect of action.
- Write organized, elaborated persuasive paper.

Sixth six weeks
- Write assessment of chosen portfolio pieces.
- Assemble/share reading/writing portfolio.

Interventions for the Student

The issue here is that the intervention be timely and occur at a classroom and a campus level. One other point is simply that for optimal learning, the student needs to stay with the regular instruction, inasmuch as possible, to have the opportunity to learn what the other students are learning. Additional time for learning must be found (e.g., using social studies time to teach non-fiction reading).

Hidden Rules

A final point is that as we work with students from all socioeconomic groups it's important to understand the hidden rules that shape how people think and who people are. The grid below gives an overview of some of the key hidden rules among the classes of poverty, middle class and wealth.

Figure G

Hidden Rules Among Classes			
	Poverty	**Middle Class**	**Wealth**
Possessions	People.	Things.	One-of-a-kind objects, legacies, pedigrees.
Money	To be used, spent.	To be managed.	To be conserved, invested.
Personality	Is for entertainment. Sense of humor is highly valued.	Is for acquisition and stability. Achievement is highly valued.	Is for connections. Financial, political, social connections are highly valued.
Social emphasis	Social inclusion of people he/she likes.	Emphasis is on self-governance and self-sufficiency.	Emphasis is on social exclusion.
Food	Key question: Did you have enough? Quantity important.	Key question: Did you like it? Quality important.	Key question: Was it presented well? Presentation important.
Clothing	Clothing valued for individual style and expression of personality.	Clothing valued for its quality and acceptance into norm of middle class. Label important.	Clothing valued for its artistic sense and expression. Designer important.
Time	Present most important. Decisions made for moment based on feelings or survival.	Future most important. Decisions made against future ramifications.	Traditions and history most important. Decisions made partially on basis of tradition and decorum.
Education	Valued and revered as abstract but not as reality.	Crucial for climbing success ladder and making money.	Necessary tradition for making and maintaining connections.
Destiny	Believes in fate. Cannot do much to mitigate chance.	Believes in choice. Can change future with good choices now.	Noblesse oblige.
Language	Casual register. Language is about survival.	Formal register. Language is about negotiation.	Formal register. Language is about networking.
Family structure	Tends to be matriarchal.	Tends to be patriarchal.	Depends on who has money.
World view	Sees world in terms of local setting.	Sees world in terms of national setting.	Sees world in terms of international view.
Love	Love and acceptance conditional, based upon whether individual is liked.	Love and acceptance conditional and based largely upon achievement.	Love and acceptance conditional and related to social standing and connections.
Driving force	Survival, relationships, entertainment	Work, achievement.	Financial, political, social connections
Humor	About people and sex	About situations.	About social faux pas.

Conclusion

What these systemic interventions allow a campus to do is to address Bloom's four variables in learning: (1) the amount of time to learn, (2) the intervention(s) of the teacher, (3) how clear the focus of the instruction is, and (4) what the student came in knowing.

This approach allows the faculty to address the amount of time, the interventions, the clarity of the instructional focus, and what the student had the opportunity to come in knowing. Right now, because of the depth and breadth of most curriculum guides, it is difficult to know what the students actually had the opportunity to learn. By having these systemic items in place, the faculty discussion can truly be data-driven; it allows the faculty to talk about student achievement in relationship to the total curriculum.

The discussion can focus on program strengths and weaknesses. It can identify areas where more time needs to be devoted and can address the effectiveness of both the whole and the component parts of the curriculum. It allows a faculty to determine staff development that will address student needs, and it provides one more tool for analyzing statewide educational data. Currently, many campuses address the test objective they were low in the year before, only to fall in other objectives the next year. This system allows a new teacher to have a much better sense of expectations. Parents also have a much better sense of the learning opportunities their children will have. It provides a tool for principals and teachers to dialogue about learning. But more importantly, it allows the campus to identify, before the damage is great, the students who aren't making sufficient progress – and to make that intervention immediately, as opposed to one or two years down the road.

This is the process I used as a principal. Our math scores made significant improvement within two years. I have used it at the secondary level in language arts with excellent results as well.

These simple models and processes give us the tools to talk about what we are doing and to minimize the unnerving roller-coaster ride for students.

References

Becoming a Nation of Readers. (1984). Center for the Study of Reading. Champaign, IL: University of Illinois.

Bloom, Benjamin. (1976). *Human Characteristics and School Learning.* New York, NY: McGraw Hill.

Fullan, Michael G. (1991). Turning systemic thinking on its head. *Phi Delta Kappan.* February. pp. 420-423.

Fullan, Michael G. (1996). *The New Meaning of Educational Change.* New York, NY: Teachers College Press, Columbia University.

BIBLIOGRAPHY

Berliner, D.C. (1988). *Implications of Studies of Expertise in Pedagogy for Teacher Education and Evaluation.* Paper presented at 1988 Educational Testing Service Invitational Conference on New Directions for Teacher Assessment. New York, NY.

Bloom, Benjamin. (1976). *Human Characteristics and School Learning.* New York, NY: McGraw-Hill Book Company.

Caine, Renate Nummela, & Caine, Geoffrey. (1991). *Making Connections: Teaching and the Human Brain.* Alexandria, VA: Association of Supervision and Curriculum Development.

Collins, Bryn C. (1997). *Emotional Unavailability: Recognizing It, Understanding It, and Avoiding Its Trap.* Lincolnwood, IL: NTC/Contemporary Publishing Company.

Covey, Stephen R. (1989). *The Seven Habits of Highly Effective People: Powerful Lessons in Personal Change.* New York, NY: Simon & Schuster.

Feuerstein, Reuven, et al. (1980). *Instrumental Enrichment: An Intervention Program for Cognitive Modifiability.* Glenview, IL: Scott, Foresman & Co.

Forward, Susan, & Frazier, Donna. (n.d.). *Emotional Blackmail.* New York, NY: HarperCollins Publishers.

Goleman, Daniel. (1995). *Emotional Intelligence.* New York, NY: Bantam Books.

Idol, Lorna, & Jones, B.F. (Eds.). (1991). *Educational Values and Cognitive Instruction: Implications for Reform.* Hillsdale, NJ: Lawrence Erlbaum Associates.

Jones, B.F., Pierce, J., & Hunter, B. (1988). Teaching students to construct graphic representations. *Educational Leadership.* Volume 46. Number 4. pp. 20-25.

Marzano, Robert J., & Arredondo, Daisy. (1986). *Tactics for Thinking.* Aurora, CO: Mid Continent Regional Educational Laboratory.

Palinscar, Anne S., & Brown, A.L. (1984). The reciprocal teaching of comprehension-fostering and comprehension-monitoring activities. *Cognition and Instruction.* Volume 1. Number 2. pp. 117-175.

Sharron, Howard, & Coulter, Martha. (1994). *Changing Children's Minds: Feuerstein's Revolution in the Teaching of Intelligence.* Exeter, Great Britain: BPC Wheatons Ltd.

Wolin, Steven J., & Wolin, Sybil. (1994). *The Resilient Self: How Survivors of Troubled Families Rise Above Adversity.* New York, NY: Villard Books.

District 220 teachers, Barrington, Illinois, used the following resources:

Carr, Eileen, & Wilson, Karen K. *Guidelines for evaluating vocabulary instruction. Journal of Reading.* Volume 29. Number 7.

Graves, Michael F., & Prenn, Maureen C. *Costs and benefits of various methods of teaching vocabulary. Journal of Reading.* Volume 29. Number 7.

Nagy, William E. (1988). *Teaching Vocabulary to Improve Reading Comprehension.* NCTE.

Stahl, Steven A. (1990). *Beyond the Instrumentalist Hypothesis: Some Relationships Between Word Meanings and Comprehension.* University of Illinois at Champaign-Urbana.

Stahl, Steven A. *Principles of effective vocabulary instruction. Journal of Reading.* Volume 29. Number 7.

aha!
Process, Inc.

www.ahaprocess.com

PO Box 727, Highlands, TX 77562-0727

FAX: (281) 426-5600

ORDER FORM

(800) 424-9484

UPS SHIP TO ADDRESS: (no post office boxes, please)

NAME:_____ E-mail _____

ORGANIZATION:_____

ADDRESS:_____

CITY/STATE/ZIP:_____

TELEPHONE: _____ FAX:_____

QTY	Title	1-4 Copies	5+ Copies	Total
	A Framework for Understanding Poverty	22.00	15.00	
	A Framework for Understanding Poverty Workbook	7.00	7.00	
	Learning Structures Workbook	7.00	7.00	
	Think Rather of Zebra	18.00	15.00	
	What Every Church Member Should Know About Poverty	22.00	15.00	
	A Picture is Worth a Thousand Words: A Developmentally Appropriate Approach to Early Learning	18.00	15.00	
	Bridges Out of Poverty: Strategies for Professionals and Communities	22.00	15.00	
	Removing the Mask: Giftedness in Poverty	25.00	20.00	
	Environmental Opportunity Profile (25/set-Incl 1 FAQ)	25.00	25.00	
	Adt'l FAQ's Environmental Opportunities Profile manual	3.00	3.00	
	Slocumb-Payne Teacher Perception Inventory (25/set)	25.00	25.00	
	Living on a Tightrope: Survival Skills for Principals	22.00	15.00	
	Preventing Violence Videos (set of 5 tapes) **S/H - $15.00**	995.00	995.00	
	Preventing Violence CD - Powerpoint Pres. **S/H - $3.00**	25.00	25.00	
	Audiotapes, Day 1 and Day 2 **S/H - $5.00**	46.00	46.00	
	Meeting Standards and Raising Test Scores When You Don't Have Much Time or Money Manuals **S/H - $6.00**	15.00	15.00	
	Meeting Standards and Raising Test Scores Resource Manuals **S/H - $6.00**	25.00	25.00	
	For Certified Trainers Only			
	A Framework for Understanding Poverty (Train the Trainers) Videos, (set of 12 tapes) **S/H - $25.00**	1995.00	1995.00	
	Audiotapes, TOT **S/H - $5.00**	125.00	125.00	
	A Framework for Understanding Poverty CD of Powerpoint Presentation **S/H - $3.00**	50.00	50.00	

Total Quantity	Subtotal	
	S/H	
	Tax	
	Total	

S/H: 1-4 books - $4.50 plus $2.00 each additional book up to 4 books
5+ books - 8% of total

TAX: 7.75% Texas residents only

Please follow these terms when ordering.

AmEx   MC   Visa   Discover

CREDIT CARD # _____ EXP DATE_____

AUTHORIZATION # _____ PO # _____